The Lake District
Youth Hosteller's Walking Guide

by

Martyn Hanks

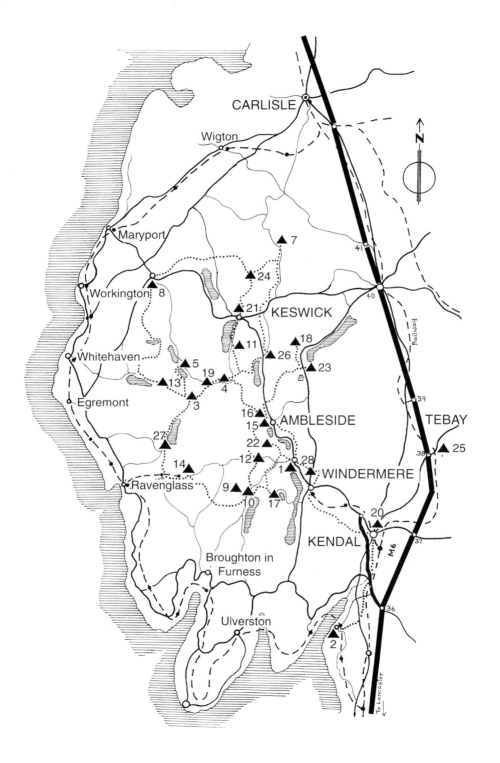

The Lake District
Youth Hosteller's Walking Guide

by

Martyn Hanks

Black Sail Hut.

Published by:
Landmark Publishing Ltd,
Waterloo House,
12 Compton, Ashbourne,
Derbyshire   DE6 1DA   England

ISBN 1 901522 26 1

British Library Cataloguing in Publication Data:
A catalogue record for this book is available from the British Library

Printed in Italy

Designed by Carreg Ltd, Ross-on-Wye, Herefordshire
Cover design: Mark Titterton Design

Acknowledgements

The publishers wish to thank the following for their assistance: Colin Logan, YHA Chief
Executive, Liz Lloyd, YHA Business Development Director, Gill Chapman, Bob Barnby
and Barbara Southam at YHA Northern Regional Office.

The text was written principally by Lindsey Porter, with assistance on the route
descriptions by Martyn Hanks.

A proportion of the royalty from each book sold is being given to the YHA Small
Hostels Fund.

**The majority of the walks in this book are low level. It is strongly recommended that
the OS map be carried on all high level walks, which should be avoided in bad
weather.**

Foreword by Colin Logan, Chief Executive
of the Youth Hostel Association of England and Wales

I am sure that many readers of this invaluable and interesting guide book will need no reminding of the importance of Youth Hostels to our National Parks and other wonderful stretches of countryside. Indeed many of you will be taking advantage of the YHA's network of accommodation in the Lake District as you read it.

Others of you may feel that you are too mature or too fond of your creature comforts to darken the doors of a Youth Hostel. Or perhaps you have only partly happy memories of school trips of many years ago and a recollection of a spartan regime in which it was mainly the shared discomfort which engendered camaraderie!

The YHA continues to serve the needs of hundreds of thousands of walkers, cyclists, schoolchildren, families, foreign backpackers and myriad other travellers every year. The accommodation remains simple and affordable by all but it is also comfortable, welcoming and well maintained. In an area such as the Lake District we offer a unique and incomparable range of experiences in terms of the location and setting of our properties.

As our President, David Bellamy, wrote last year "While others have recently discovered the concept of sustainable tourism, our aim from the start has been to instill knowledge and love for the countryside, and an understanding of the deeper values associated with our environment and heritage".

Much of the time you may be more concerned with the tiredness in your legs or the shortness of your breath. But when you pause to take in the fantastic landscape views which the walks described in this book offer you, I am sure that you will think of these deeper values - as indeed you will when you arrive at a Youth Hostel after your strenuous day out and enjoy the warmth of hospitality and companionship to be found there.

I hope that you enjoy this guide and find the walks from it to be rewarding.

CDC Logan

THE WALKS

THE YOUTH HOSTELS

N.B. Figures in brackets refer to the numbers on the map
opposite the title page

What is the YHA?

"To help all, especially young people of limited means, to a greater love and care of the countryside, particularly by providing hostels or other simple accommodation for them in their travels, and thus to promote their health, rest and education". These aims, set out when the Youth Hostels Association first began in 1930, remain as important as ever. The Association grew from the dedicated effort of visionary people and provided a firm foundation for recent years which has seen great strides in upgrading and the development of new hostels.

Images are often outdated — of spartan surroundings, rules and regulations and a belief that hostels are only for young people. Today, a youth hostel signifies good value accommodation which is friendly, comfortable, dependable and secure, backed up by an assurance of standards which apply to youth hostels around the world.

The 242 youth hostels throughout England and Wales provide a major national re-source. Together they account for over 14,000 bedspaces which places the YHA in the top league of accommodation providers. But it is the location of the hostels which makes them a truly unique asset. Over the years, sites have been found in some of our most spectacular landscapes, in remote hill country, on Heritage coasts, or lowland woodland settings. Many youth hostels are in villages or small towns, where they are close to the countryside but also are accessible to other facilities and form part of the local community. The hostels in the Lake District range in size and character from rustic mountain huts to grand Lakeside mansions; many are in incomparable locations ideal for walkers.

As a body of some 270,000 members in England and Wales, the YHA is a social movement, enabling people of all ages to meet others in a special atmosphere of friend-ship. The International movement, of which YHA England & Wales forms a part, is rightly seen as a force for peace and understanding. Membership of YHA England & Wales entitles people to travel and hostel in over 60 countries around the world with more than 5,000 Youth Hostels to choose from.

Whilst others have recently discovered the concept of "sustainable tourism", the aim of the YHA from the start has been to instill a knowledge and love for the countryside and an understanding of the deeper values associated with our environment and heritage. This has always come first; our accommodation is a means to this end. Increasingly, there is a wide range of types of hostel, clearly indicated so that members can select which one is likely to meet their particular needs. Yet throughout, our firm principle is that the simple, recognisable character of youth hostels is always retained.

From its inception, the YHA has been an environmental movement which has worked with its own resources to implement sustainable tourism principles in practice. We have a seven point Environmental Charter for Youth Hostels world wide which underlines our commitment to important issues such as reducing consumption, recycling and conserving energy.

The 26 youth hostels in the Lake District exemplify the YHA with their wide range of opportunities to explore all parts from the bustling market and lakeside towns to the remote and little visited upper fells. The YHA is a membership organisation and you will be asked to show your membership card on arrival at a youth hostel. If you are not already a member, you can join at the first youth hostel you visit or alternatively contact YHA for a membership form (you will find a special voucher entitling you to a free one year's membership on the last page of this book). You will receive a free annual guide listing all the hostels in England & Wales and receive a regular members' magazine and discounts on travel, places of interest and shops.

Booking your stay is easy — simply telephone or write to the Ambleside Youth Hostel booking bureau 015394 32304. Even travelling between hostels in the Lake District is made easy with the help of the YHA shuttle bus, a hostel door to door service which carries you and your backpack to certain hostels. The bus also meets most trains at Windermere Railway Station.

When you stay at a youth hostel you will sleep in comfortable bunk bedded rooms sharing with people of the same sex, unless you have made special arrangements in advance — for instance, families or groups of friends may be able to have their own private bunkroom. More and more youth hostels now offer rooms with fewer beds, often with their own washing facilities. Otherwise, you will find showers, toilets and washing facilities close to your room. You will be given freshly laundered bed linen with which to make up your bed. Pillows, duvets and/or blankets are also provided.

At most youth hostels you will find comfortable sitting areas for relaxing and socialising, as well as facilities such as drying rooms, cycle stores and local information. While many hostels have areas specially set aside for smoking, there are also many "No Smoking" hostels. At smaller youth hostels — to keep prices low — you may be asked to help with simple household tasks. You are asked to clear up after yourself.

Circular routes from a hostel are popular with walkers who like to spend several nights in one place, exploring the countryside from their base. If you are a member of a walking club or simply a group of friends and family you can choose in the winter to rent a whole youth hostel for your group under the YHA's Rent-a-Hostel scheme. Some of the smaller youth hostels in the Lake District are available — with a key for you to come and go as you please and good self-catering facilities for all your meals. A brochure on Rent-a-Hostel explains how to book.

YHA has been spending considerable sums of money refurbishing its buildings and improving standards of comfort and privacy. Each year, more hostels are identified for improvement, a few more properties open for business for the first time , and those surplus to requirements are closed.

Today YHA is a vibrant organisation catering for the needs of young and old. So long as you are young at heart, a warm welcome awaits you!

Liz Lloyd
Business Development Director, YHA

THE WALKS

Walking route Ambleside YH to Elterwater YH
(The map is on pages 14/15)

Take Borran's Road beyond the steamer jetty. The route follows the River Rothay and Under Loughrigg Road out of town before climbing uphill onto the east flank of Loughrigg Fell. The path soon gains in height before becoming much easier as the fell is crossed. The path descends to Little Loughrigg just to the south of Loughrigg Tarn before reaching Skelwith Bridge. The alternative route shown is more direct, climbing up past Lily Tarn on a steeper route. From Skelwith Bridge, the path is fairly flat and easy. It passes Skelwith Force (waterfall) and then Elter Water on part of the Cumbria Way, before reaching Elterwater village by the bridge and carpark.

Walking route Ambleside YH to Hawkshead YH
(The maps are on pages 16/19)

This route follows the Elterwater route as far as Skelwith Bridge. It then follows the Cumbria Way on an easy path before crossing the A593 and following an old lane towards Tarn Hows. The lake here, especially when viewed from the south side, is most attractive. It is perhaps the most popular spot in Lakeland, irrespective of the season. If time allows, there is a circular route around the lake, so you can take the longer way around if you prefer.

The path climbs up and away from the Tarn, cutting through a wood before reaching the road from Knipe Fold, just after passing Hill Cottage. Upon reaching the hamlet of Hawkshead Hill, the B5285 is followed for a few yards before a path to the right leads directly to Hawkshead village. Head for the church if you wish to go into the village, otherwise follow the path and lane shown on the map to reach the youth hostel.

Walks around Ambleside YH
(The maps are on pages 20/23)

This consists of both a low and high level route. The latter is not recommended in bad weather unless you are well equipped with protective clothing.

The **low level route** heads for the River Rothay along Borran's Road, passing the remains of the Roman fort in the park just beyond the steamer jetty. It follows under Loughrigg Road which runs adjacent to the river all the way to Rydal village. Here you can cross the ancient bridge and walk up the path adjacent to the A591 into Rydal to visit

Rydal Mount, the last home of William Wordsworth. His former house is behind the hall which is visible over the wall running up the side of the A591. Alternatively you can continue on by Rydal Water or Loughrigg Terrace (past Rydal Cave) to reach Grasmere lake and village.

There is a return low level path which passes Dove Cottage (another Wordsworth home) and, on gaining an elevated level above the valley, contours around to Rydal. It then runs through Rydal Park to Scandale Bridge on the outskirts of Ambleside.

The **high level** path follows the Ambleside to Elterwater route from Clappersgate, and then rises to the north of Ivy Crag to the top of Loughrigg at 1,099ft (338m) before descending to Grasmere via Loughrigg Terrace.

There are several short walks around the town which are especially ideal for summer evenings.

Walk into Ambleside and at the Garden Centre, cross the road and go up Old Lake Road. Then turn right up Skelghyll Lane. This brings you to Skelghyll Woods and the view point at Jenkin Crag. A path returns to the hostel adjacent to Stagshaw Gardens which are worthy of a visit if time permits.

From the centre of town, take Stock Ghyll Road and then take the path to see the waterfall in Stock Ghyll Park. You can return down the road and leave town along Vicarage Road to reach Rothay Park. Having crossed the river, turn left along Under Loughrigg Road to reach Borrans Road which brings you back to Waterhead and the youth hostel.

Ambleside YH to Windermere YH

(The map is on pages 24/25)

This route can also be used as part of a day's circular walk from either youth hostel (here it starts, for convenience, from Ambleside).

Take the lane opposite the Esso garage adjacent to the hostel on the A591. It climbs up through Skelghyll Wood to the viewpoint at Jenkin Crag where you can stop to enjoy the lake view. On leaving the wood, the path goes through High Skelghyll Farm. On crossing Hol Beck, the path climbs uphill again to join a track known as Robin Lane which drops down into Troutbeck village. Town End House is owned by the National Trust and open to visitors. Windermere YH is a short distance to the south on the Troutbeck Bridge road.

From Troutbeck, the path returns to Ambleside via Wansfell, climbing about 1,000ft (308m). It starts up Nanny Lane near the Mortal Man Inn. There are superb views from the top. The route then descends down to Stock Ghyll Park where the impressive waterfall can be seen before returning to the youth hostel through the streets of Ambleside.

Ambleside YH to Langdale YH

(The map is on pages 26/27)

The path follows the road past the steamer jetty to the A593. It passes the remains of the Roman fort in the park to your left. The River Rothey is followed along Under Loughrigg Road before climbing up onto Loughrigg Fell and heading to Ivy Crag. The path skirts around the south side of the latter before descending towards Loughrigg Tarn. It remains on relatively level ground, rising a little north of the tarn as one approaches Langdale YH. This path combines a short distance of fell walking with a much gentler walk to finish off.

Alternative routes are available including the ascent of Loughrigg and via Rydal — walks already covered under **Walks around Ambleside** above.

WORDSWORTH'S LAKE DISTRICT

Rydal Water from White Moss Common

Photo: Alex Black

"Here the rainbow comes - the cloud - And mists that spread the flying shroud..."

WORDSWORTH HOUSE
Cockermouth

The house where William Wordsworth was born in 1770. Seven rooms are furnished in 18th-century style, with some personal effects of the poet; his childhood garden, with terraced walk leads down to the River Derwent. Kitchen restaurant, Shop, Events during the season.
Open: Mar 26 - Nov 1,
weekdays (inc. Saturdays, Mar 29, May 3 & 24 &
all Sats June 28 to Sept 6, Oct 25 and Nov 1).
(National Trust)

TEL: 01900 824805

DOVE COTTAGE
Grasmere

Dove Cottage & Wordsworth Museum, Grasmere
Open Daily 9.30 to 5.30pm.
Closed 24th - 26th December

Parking next to Dove Cottage Tearoom &
Vegetarian Restaurant immediately south
of Grasmere village.

TEL: 015394 35544/35547

RYDAL MOUNT
Near Ambleside

Rydal Mount Home of William
Wordsworth from 1813 - 1850
Open:
Summer: Mar - Oct 9.30 - 5.00pm
Winter: Nov - Feb 10.00 - 4.00pm
(Closed Tuesdays in Winter)

FREE PARKING

TEL: 015394 33002

RECIPROCAL DISCOUNT OFFER - DETAILS FROM ANY OF THE ABOVE ATTRACTIONS

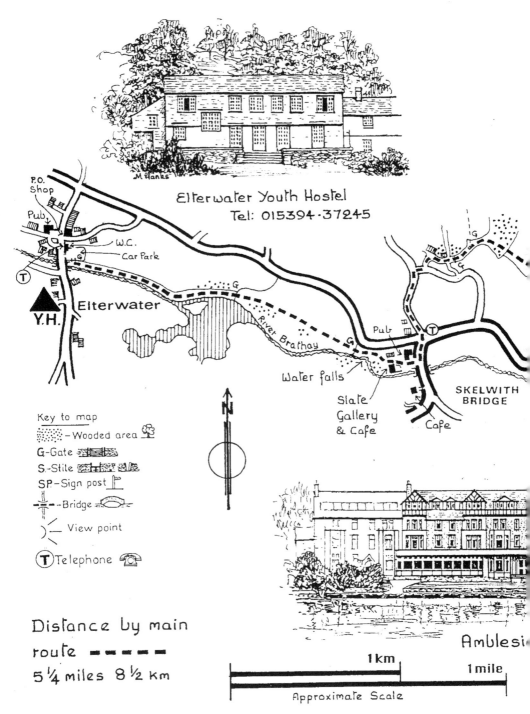

Elterwater Youth Hostel
Tel: 015394·37245

P.O. Shop
Pub
W.C.
Car Park
Elterwater
T
Y.H.
River Brathay
Water falls
Slate Gallery & Cafe
Pub
T
Cafe
SKELWITH BRIDGE

Key to map
░ – Wooded area
G – Gate
S. – Stile
SP – Sign post
– Bridge
View point
T Telephone

Amblesi

Distance by main
route ▬ ▬ ▬ ▬
5¼ miles 8½ km

1 km
1 mile
Approximate Scale

14

Walking route between
Ambleside YH and Elterwater YH

see page 10

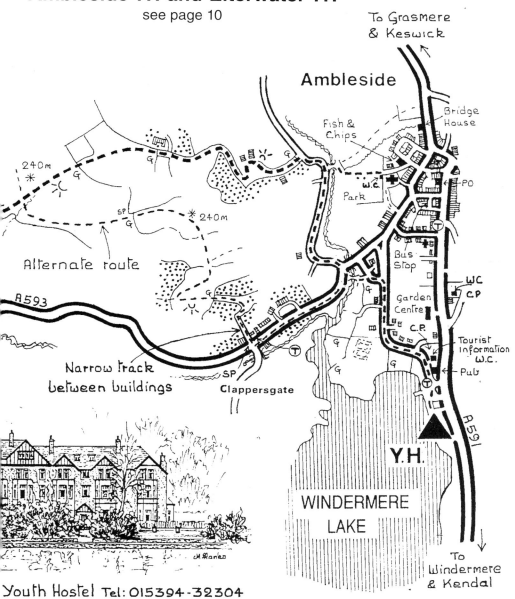

To Grasmere & Keswick

Ambleside

Bridge House

Fish & Chips

240m

G

SP

240m

Alternate route

A593

Narrow track between buildings

Clappersgate

Park

W.C.

PO

Bus Stop

WC
C.P.

Garden Centre

C.P.

Tourist Information
W.C.

Pub

A591

Y.H.

WINDERMERE LAKE

To Windermere & Kendal

Youth Hostel Tel: 015394-32304

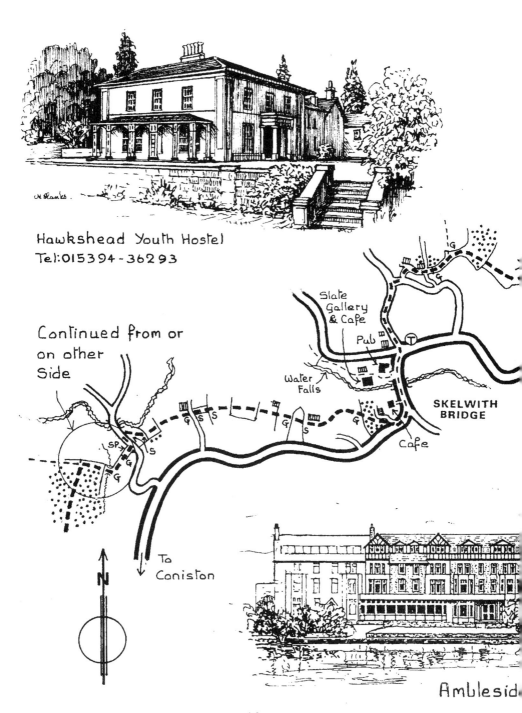

Hawkshead Youth Hostel
Tel: 015394 - 36293

Continued from or
on other
Side

Slate
Gallery
& Cafe

Pub

Water
Falls

SKELWITH
BRIDGE

Cafe

To
Coniston

N

Ambleside

Walking route between
Ambleside YH and Hawkshead YH: Map 1

see page 10

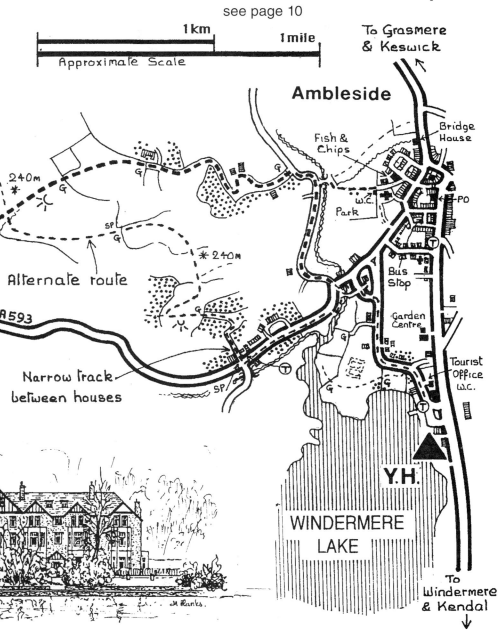

1 km

1 mile

Approximate Scale

To Grasmere & Keswick

Ambleside

Bridge House

Fish & Chips

240m

G

W.C.

PO

Park

Bus Stop

Alternate route

240m

A593

Garden Centre

Narrow track between houses

SP

Tourist Office W.C.

Y.H.

WINDERMERE LAKE

To Windermere & Kendal

M Ranks.

Hostel Tel: 015394-32304

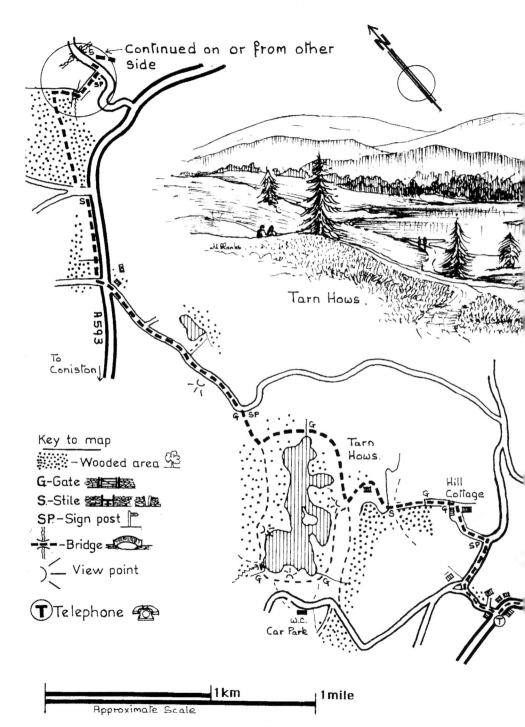

Continued on or from other side

Tarn Hows.

A593

To Coniston

Tarn Hows.

Hill Cottage

Key to map

- Wooded area
G - Gate
S - Stile
SP - Sign post
- Bridge
- View point
T Telephone

W.C.
Car Park

1 km   1 mile
Approximate Scale

18

Walking route between
Ambleside YH and Hawkshead YH: Map 2

see page 10

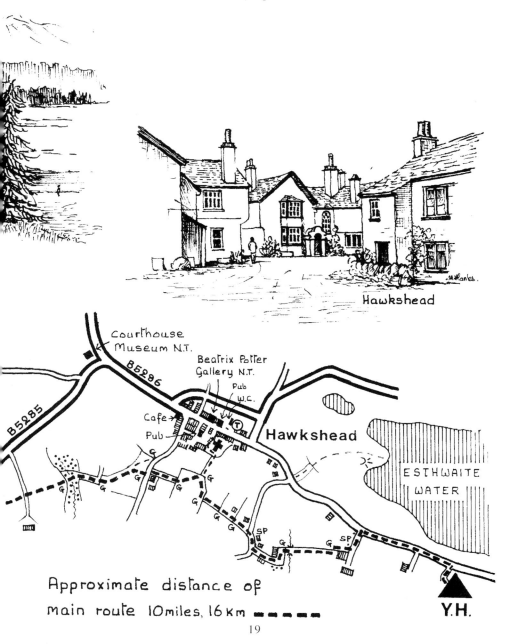

Hawkshead

Courthouse Museum N.T.

B5286

Beatrix Potter Gallery N.T.

Pub

W.C.

B5285

Cafe

Pub

Hawkshead

ESTHWAITE WATER

SP

SP

Approximate distance of
main route 10 miles, 16 km ▬ ▬ ▬ ▬

Y.H.

19

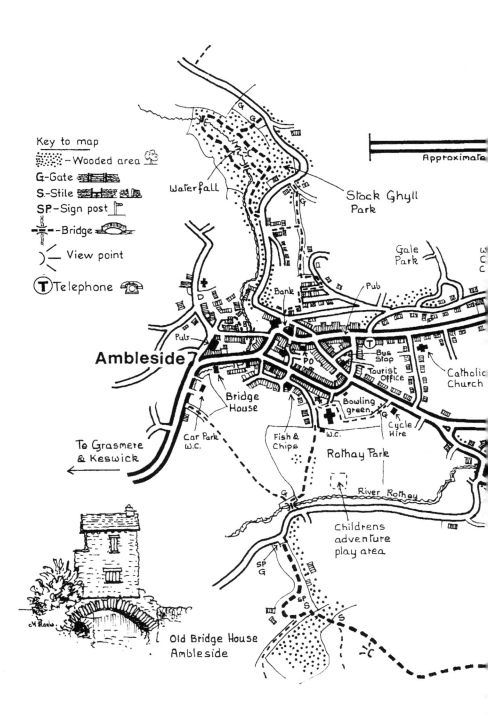

Key to map

░░░ – Wooded area

G – Gate

S – Stile

SP – Sign post

– Bridge

View point

T Telephone

Waterfall

Stock Ghyll Park

Gale Park

Bank

Pub

Pub

Ambleside

Bus Stop

Tourist Office

Catholic Church

PO

Bridge House

Bowling green

Cycle Hire

To Grasmere & Keswick

Car Park W.C.

Fish & Chips

W.C.

Rothay Park

River Rothay

Childrens adventure play area

SP G

SP S

S

Old Bridge House Ambleside

Approximate

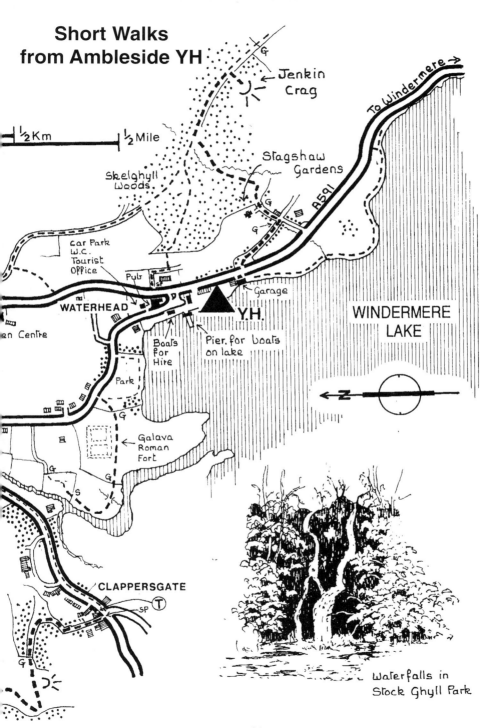

Short Walks from Ambleside YH

Jenkin Crag

To Windermere →

½Km ½Mile

Stagshaw Gardens

Skelghyll Woods.

A591

Car Park
W.C.
Tourist
Office

Pub

Garage

WATERHEAD

en Centre

Boats for Hire

Pier. for boats on lake

Y.H.

WINDERMERE LAKE

Park

N

Galava Roman Fort

CLAPPERSGATE

SP Ⓣ

Waterfalls in Stock Ghyll Park

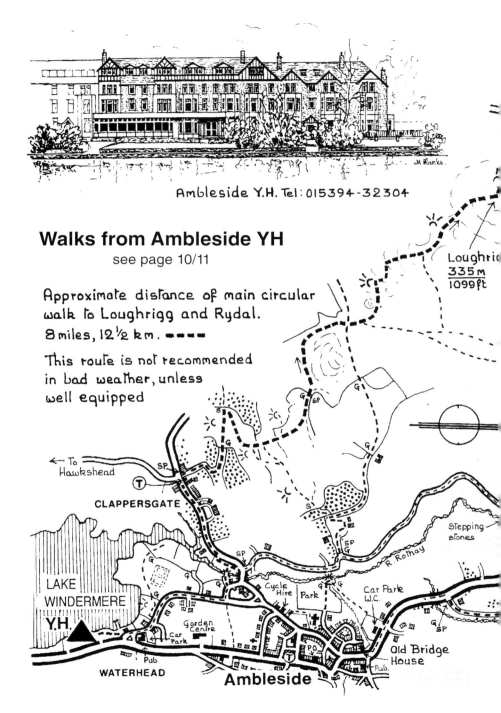

Ambleside Y.H. Tel: 015394-32304

Walks from Ambleside YH

see page 10/11

Approximate distance of main circular walk to Loughrigg and Rydal. 8 miles, 12½ km. ▬ ▬ ▬ ▬

This route is not recommended in bad weather, unless well equipped

Loughrig
335 m
1099 ft

← To Hawkshead

CLAPPERSGATE

Stepping stones

R. Rothay

LAKE WINDERMERE

Cycle Hire   Park

Car Park W.C.

Y.H. ▲

Garden Centre

Car Park

Old Bridge House

Pub

WATERHEAD

Ambleside

Pub.

22

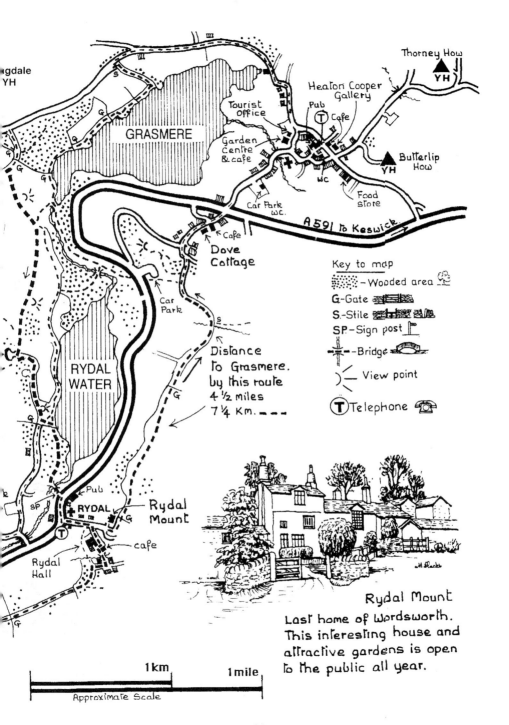

gdale
YH

Thorney How
YH

GRASMERE

Heaton Cooper
Gallery

Tourist
Office

Pub

T Cafe

Butterlip
How
YH

Garden
Centre
& cafe

WC

Food
store

Car Park
WC

A591 to Keswick

Cafe

Dove
Cottage

Car
Park

RYDAL
WATER

Key to map

⬚⬚⬚ - Wooded area 🌳

G - Gate

S. - Stile

SP - Sign post

✛ - Bridge 🌉

) (- View point

T Telephone ☎

Distance
to Grasmere.
by this route
4 ½ miles
7 ¼ Km. ---

S

G

Pub

SP

RYDAL

Rydal
Mount

T

cafe

Rydal
Hall

G

Rydal Mount

Last home of Wordsworth.
This interesting house and
attractive gardens is open
to the public all year.

1km

1mile

Approximate Scale

23

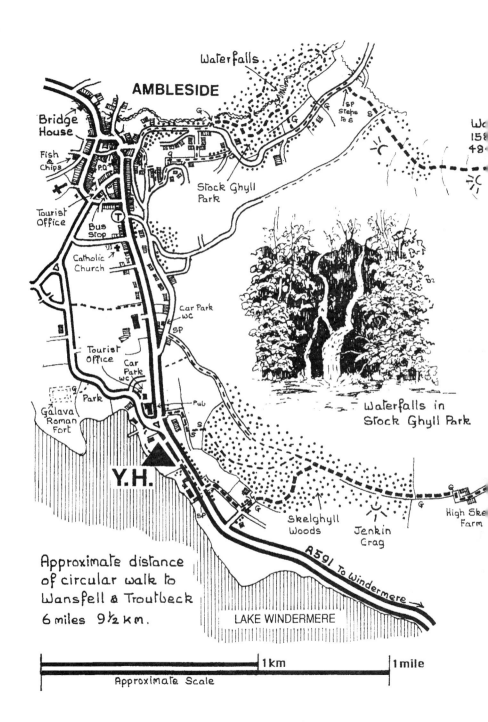

Circular Walk from Ambleside YH
(via Windermere YH)

page 12

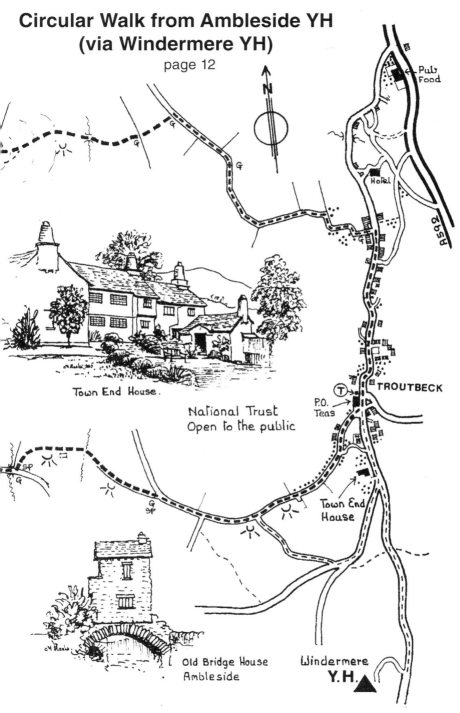

N

Pub
Food

Hotel

A592

Town End House.

National Trust
Open to the public

P.O.
Teas

TROUTBECK

SP
G

G
SP

Town End
House

Old Bridge House
Ambleside

Windermere
Y.H.

25

Walking route between Ambleside YH and Langdale YH

see page 12

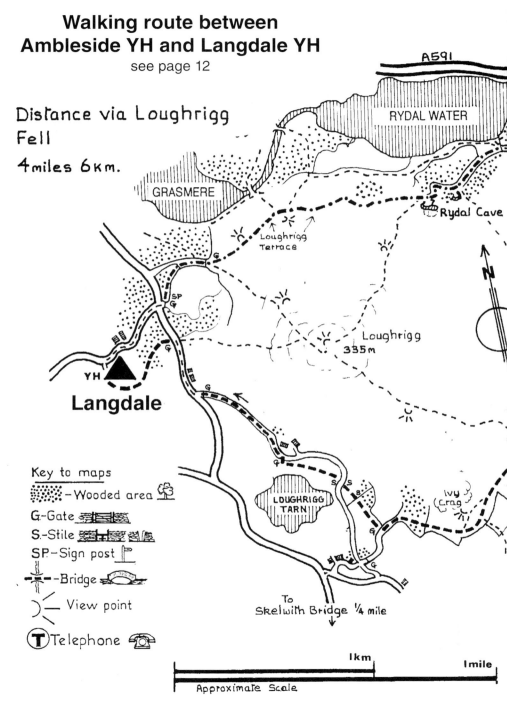

Distance via Loughrigg Fell

4 miles 6 km.

A591

RYDAL WATER

GRASMERE

Rydal Cave

Loughrigg Terrace

Loughrigg 335m

N

YH

Langdale

Key to maps

:::::: - Wooded area

G-Gate

S.-Stile

SP-Sign post

-Bridge

View point

(T) Telephone

LOUGHRIGG TARN

Ivy Crag

To Skelwith Bridge ¼ mile

1 km

1 mile

Approximate Scale

26

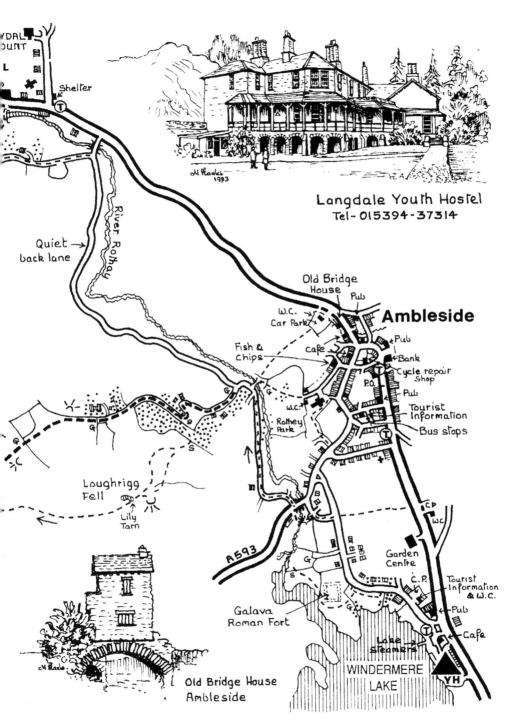

Langdale Youth Hostel
Tel- 015394-37314

Shelter

Quiet back lane

River Rothay

Old Bridge House
Pub

Ambleside

W.C.
Car Park

Fish & Chips

Café

Pub

Bank

Cycle repair Shop

P.O.

Pub

W.C.

Rothay Park

Tourist Information

Bus stops

Loughrigg Fell

Lily Tarn

A593

C.P.

W.C.

Garden Centre

C.P.

Tourist Information & W.C.

Pub

Cafe

Galava Roman Fort

Lake Steamers

WINDERMERE LAKE

YH

Old Bridge House
Ambleside

Walks from Langdale YH

(The maps are on pages 30/33)

Langdale YH is situated in an area of magnificent scenery, both in Langdale itself and around Grasmere. The walks recommended here are relatively short and low level. The nearby Lakeland Fells offer superb walking for the more experienced. The hostel is close to Elterwater which can be reached by lanes. From the carpark in Elterwater village, the river (the Great Langdale Beck) can be followed down to Elter Water and on to Skelwith Bridge, returning via Loughrigg Tarn. This can be extended by following the lane beyond Elterwater YH to Little Langdale, then taking the path to Slater Bridge near Little Langdale Tarn. The route then heads eastwards down the valley, joining the Cumbria Way near Colwith Force waterfall. This extends the path from 4 to 7.5 miles (6.4-12km).

A further extension of this leaves the above path just beyond Slater Bridge. It goes through Moss Rigg Wood and above the Pierce How Beck, heading for Tilberthwaite. Despite a lot of mining and quarrying here, this is a lovely area. From Tilberthwaite there are roads running down each side of the river towards the Coniston-Ambleside road (A593).

The path joins the A593 for a short distance before climbing from near Yew Tree Tarn over Tom Heights to reach Tarn Hows. Join the path which leads around the lake and leave it at its northern end to reach a lane which descends towards the A593 again. On passing through a wood, the Little Langdale to Skelwith Bridge path is rejoined. Although extending the walking to a total of 11 miles (17km) in total, the additional distance takes you through some superb scenery.

Grasmere to Borrowdale and Honister Hause YHs

(The maps are on pages 34/37)

Both of the Grasmere hostels are situated conveniently off Easedale Road which is followed to Lancrigg. Here the path climbs up towards a wood and then passes below disused quarries. Above, the side of Helm Crag climbs steeply to 1,299ft (400m). An alternative high level ridge walk from Helm Crag (it is shown on the map) can be taken with views to Grasmere Common, the Langdales, Helvellyn, Loughrigg etc. It is shown on the map.

The lower path proceeds up Far Easedale Gill below Moment Crag heading for the open moorland northwest of High Raise. This is likely to be boggy in places. The path turns northwest upon reaching Greenup Edge and then follows a steep climb up a gully at Lining Crag before the hardwork slips behind you! Ahead, Greenup Gill descends towards Stonethwaite. The valley narrows and levels off on reaching the junction with the Langstrath Valley.

Even if you wish to reach the pub and café in Stonethwaite, ignore the footbridges for there is a bridge in the village. Beyond the village, the valley widens out as it reaches Borrowdale and Rosthwaite. Your route is down the lane with Borrowdale hostel just across the B5289 at Longthwaite.

For the onward trip to Honister, a path climbs up the valley above Seatoller village. It's a stiff climb the whole way, gaining about 800ft (246m) in height. The hostel is right at the summit of the Pass!

Grasmere to Elterwater and Coniston YHs

(The maps are on pages 38/41)

This path follows in part the circular **walks around Langdale** and crosses through some wonderful scenery.

It leaves the road near to the boat hire jetty, up an unpaved lane (in spring look for the daffodils up on the left). The route climbs steadily uphill with Silver How to the right. It drops down to Chapel Stile, with its cottages hugging the side of the fell.

It's a short walk down the beck to Elterwater with the Langdale time-share village across the stream. The route to Coniston continues by taking the lane just beyond the Elterwater YH. It leads to Little Langdale, Slater Bridge and via Moss Rigg Wood to Tilberthwaite. There is a lane either side of the beck from here. The left hand side shown on the map is the quieter one.

After crossing the A593 (Yewdale Road) the route crosses the fields to Coniston village. If you want a higher level route to reach Coniston, a path climbs up Tilberthwaite Gill beneath the high fells and above Yewdale Beck. Opposite, the tips of an old mine and quarry still disfigure the valley side. The route turns south below the Furness Fells heading for Coniston Copper Mines YH and the Levers Water Beck. This section and the first section to Chapel Stile are not recommended in poor weather.

The circular walks below Grasmere have been described under Langdale owing to the close proximity of the hostels. However a further recommended walk to Alcock Tarn starts from the Swan Inn on the A591 at the northern outskirts of Grasmere. It climbs up the side of Heron Pike opposite the village before heading south for the elongated tarn. From here it passes Grey Crag and descends to the lane above Dove Cottage. It is only 3.5 miles (5.5km) in length. It climbs about 1,000ft (300m) to the tarn and is not recommended in poor weather.

Starting virtually opposite Thorney How YH a path runs up Easedale to Easedale Tarn. It's a fairly easy walk and there is a a circular walk around the tarn. The route returns via Far Easedale Gill to join the track which runs back to Grasmere beneath Helm Crag.

Walks from Langdale YH

see page 28

Key to maps
- ▓ – Wooded area
- G – Gate
- S – Stile
- SP – Sign post
- – Bridge
- View point
- T Telephone

Distance of walks

Circular walk to
Elterwater & Skelwith Br
4 miles 6½ km in total

Circular to Slater Br
7½ miles 12 km in total

Circular to Tarn Hows 11 miles 17 km in total

These are all low level routes ideal for bad weather

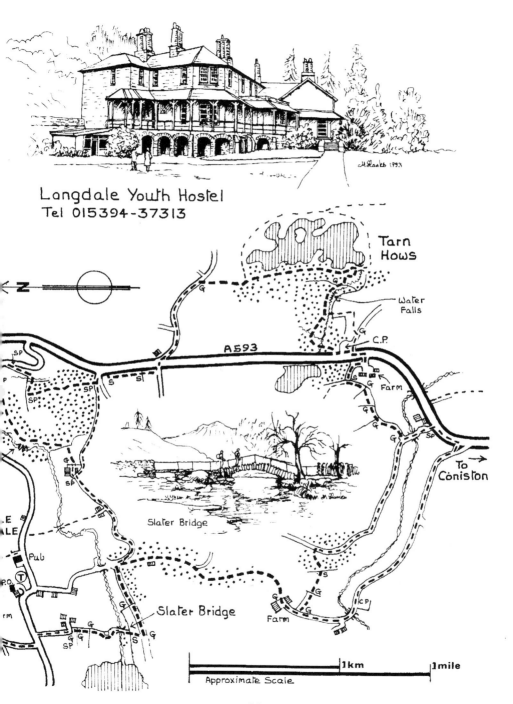

Langdale Youth Hostel
Tel 015394-37313

Tarn
Hows

Water
Falls

N

A593

C.P.

SP

P

SP

SP

S S

Farm

Slater Bridge

To
Coniston

E
LE

Pub

P.O. T

rm

SP

Slater Bridge

Farm

C.P

1km   1mile

Approximate Scale

31

Walks from Langdale YH

see page 28

High level walk to Grasmere
and back to Y.H. ▬·▬·▬
5 miles 8 km.
This route is poorly defined
in places and should only
be made in good weather
Take compass.

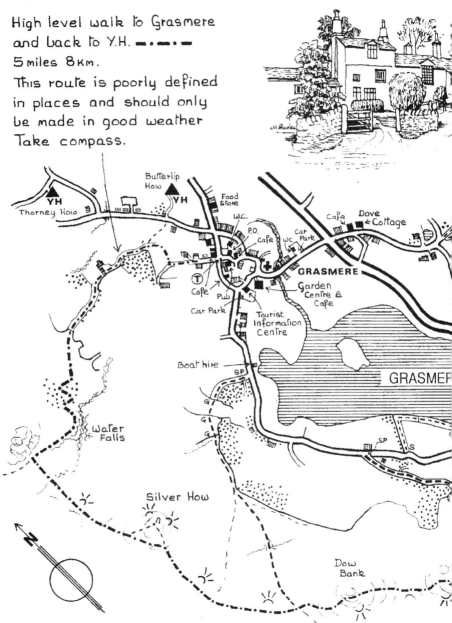

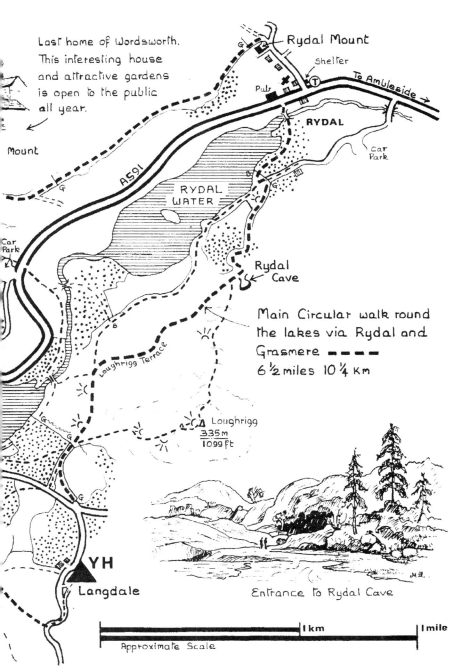

Last home of Wordsworth. This interesting house and attractive gardens is open to the public all year.

Rydal Mount

Shelter

To Ambleside →

Mount

Pub

A591

RYDAL

Car Park

RYDAL WATER

Car Park

Rydal Cave

Main Circular walk round the lakes via Rydal and Grasmere ━ ━ ━
6½ miles 10¼ km

Loughrigg Terrace

Loughrigg
335m
1099ft

YH
Langdale

Entrance to Rydal Cave

1 km   1 mile

Approximate Scale

33

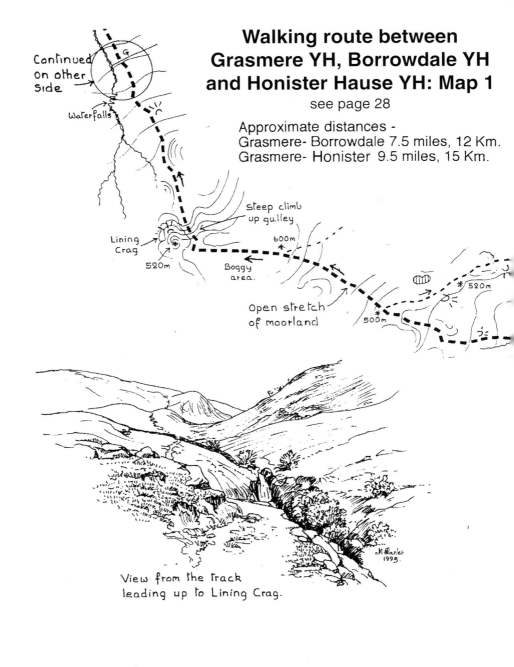

Walking route between Grasmere YH, Borrowdale YH and Honister Hause YH: Map 1

see page 28

Approximate distances -
Grasmere- Borrowdale 7.5 miles, 12 Km.
Grasmere- Honister 9.5 miles, 15 Km.

Continued on other Side

G

Waterfalls

Steep climb up gulley

600m

Lining Crag

520m

Boggy area.

Open stretch of moorland

500m

520m

View from the track leading up to Lining Crag.

M Clarke 1995.

1km   1mile

Approximate Scale

Thorney How Youth Hostel. Grasmere
Tel - 015394 - 35591

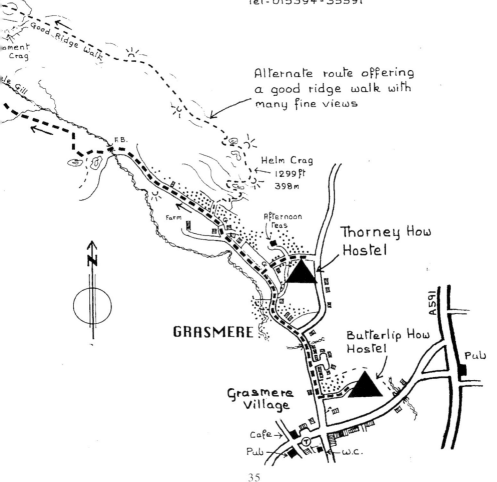

Good Ridge Walk

Alternate route offering
a good ridge walk with
many fine views

ament Crag

le Gill

F.B.

Helm Crag
1299 ft
398 m

Farm

Afternoon
Teas

Thorney How
Hostel

GRASMERE

A591

Butterlip How
Hostel

Pub

Grasmere
Village

Cafe →
Pub → ⓉⓉ → W.C.

35

Walking route between Grasmere YH, Borrowdale YH and Honister Hause YH: Map 2

see page 28

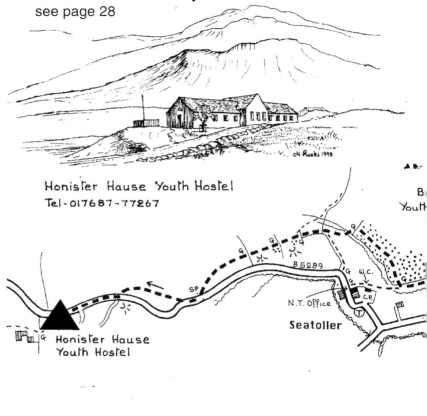

Honister Hause Youth Hostel
Tel-017687-77267

Honister Hause
Youth Hostel

Stonethwaite village from the bridge

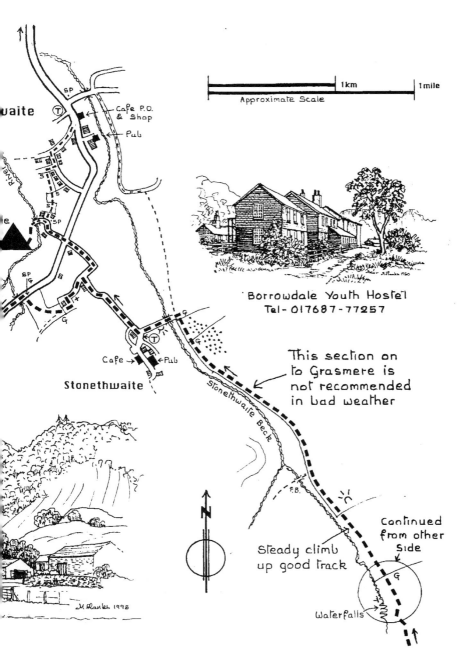

waite

Cafe P.O. & Shop

Pub

1km   1mile

Approximate Scale

Borrowdale Youth Hostel
Tel- 017687-77257

This section on to Grasmere is not recommended in bad weather

Cafe →   ←Pub

Stonethwaite

Stonethwaite Beck

N

Steady climb up good track

F.B.

Continued from other side

Waterfalls

M. Planks 1998

37

Walking route between
Grasmere YH, Elterwater YH and Coniston YH: Map
see page 29

1km   1 mile

Approximate Scale

Approximate distances

Grasmere to Coniston
Holly How 9¼ miles 14¾ km.

Coppermines 10½ miles 16¾ km.

Elterwater 4½ miles 7¼ km

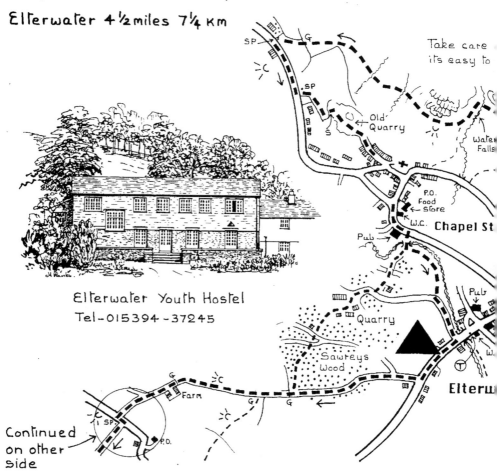

Elterwater Youth Hostel
Tel-015394-37245

Continued
on other
side

38

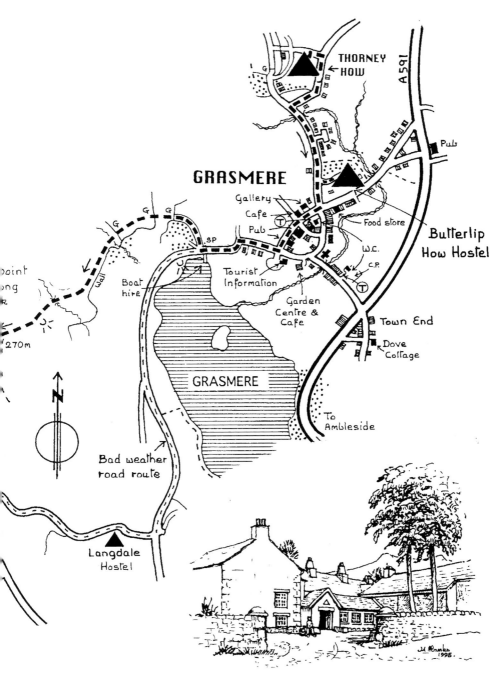

THORNEY HOW

A591

GRASMERE

Gallery
Cafe
Pub

Food store

Butterlip
How Hostel

W.C.

Pub

C.P.

point
ong

Boat
hire

Tourist
Information

Garden
Centre &
Cafe

Town End

Dove
Cottage

270m

Wall

N

GRASMERE

To
Ambleside

Bad weather
road route

Langdale
Hostel

Thorney How Youth Hostel. Grasmere
Tel·015394-35591

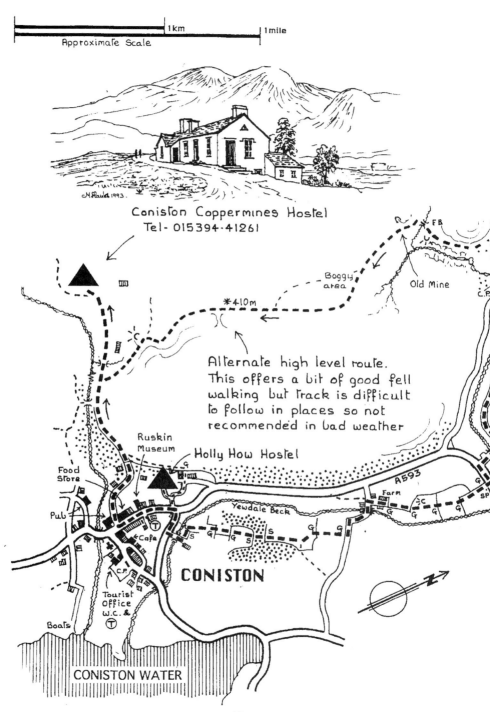

Approximate Scale

Coniston Coppermines Hostel
Tel- 015394·41261

FB

Boggy area

Old Mine

C.P.

* 410m

Alternate high level route.
This offers a bit of good fell
walking but track is difficult
to follow in places so not
recommended in bad weather

Ruskin Museum

Holly How Hostel

Food Store

A593

Farm

Pub

Yewdale Beck

Cafe

CONISTON

C.P.

Tourist Office W.C. &

Boats

CONISTON WATER

Walking route between
Grasmere YH, Elterwater YH and Coniston YH: Map 2
see page 29

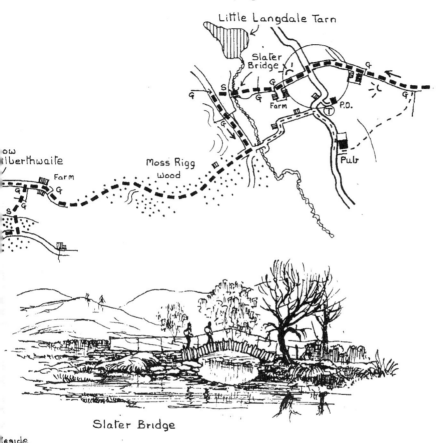

Slater Bridge

Coniston Holly How Hostel Tel·015394·41

Around Langdale and Grasmere

(The maps are on pages 44/47)

A walk up the road beyond the hostel brings you to a path which leads down to the Grasmere road. Upon reaching the road you are on the route described under **Walks around Ambleside**.

From Grasmere, the route proceeds to Rydal Mount, with views across Rydal Water to Loughrigg. It returns via Loughrigg Terrace. From Martyn Hank's map you can see variations, such as the path between Grasmere lake and Rydal Water which reduces the walk, or over Loughrigg which is more arduous.

A further high level route climbs up from the hostel to Dow Bank and Silver How before dropping down into Grasmere. This has wonderful views across to Rydal Fell and Great Rigg, but is poorly defined in places and should only be attempted by experienced walkers. A deviation after passing Dow Bank brings you down to the boat jetty on Grasmere lake.

Coniston YH to Hawkshead YH

(The map is on pages 48/49)

Leaving Coniston, the path runs through the fields close to the Yewdale Beck and the A593 road to Ambleside. It leaves the valley to climb up to Tarn Hows where there is a circular path around the tarn if preferred. The direct route proceeds around the south side of the tarn (with the benefit of the best view) and climbs up to Hawkshead Hill before crossing the fields to Hawkshead village.

Elterwater YH to Hawkshead YH

(The map is on pages 50/51)

A choice of two routes is given, each approximately of the same distance 7.5 miles (12km). One route goes down to Skelwith Bridge past Elter Water, to join the Cumbria Way at that point. The other route goes to Slater Bridge, with both routes coming together on the A593 road shortly before you cross the latter and head for Tarn Hows. The route then follows the Ambleside-Hawkshead route to reach Hawkshead YH.

Coniston YH to Ambleside YH

(The maps are on pages 52/55)

The path along the Yewdale Beck is followed with the pronounced Yewdale Crag on your left. On reaching the A593 either turn left for Tilberthwaite or head for Tarn Hows. The former route proceeds on a well used path from Tilberthwaite above the Pierce How Beck to the ford near to Little Langdale Tarn. Here it joins a track to skirt Great How before reaching Tongue Intake Plantation, owned by the National Trust.

Here the path via Tarn Hows is reached (for detail see **Walks around Langdale YH).** The path follows the Cumbria Way through the fields to Skelwith Bridge and then ascends Loughrigg Fell before dropping down into Ambleside. This section of the route is described under **Ambleside YH to Elterwater YH.**

Walks around Langdale YH and Grasmere YH

see page 42

Circular walk to Rydal is low level on good paths. Distance 6½ miles 9½ Km in total.

Walk to Alcock Tarn. 3½ miles 5½ Km in total. Not recommended in bad weather

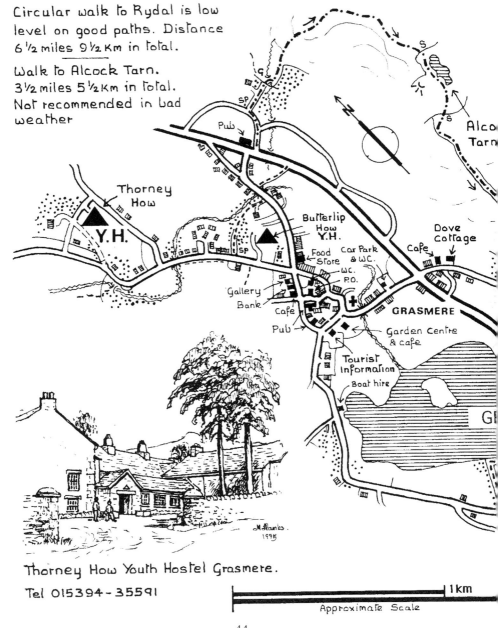

Thorney How Youth Hostel Grasmere.

Tel 015394-35591

1 km

Approximate Scale

44

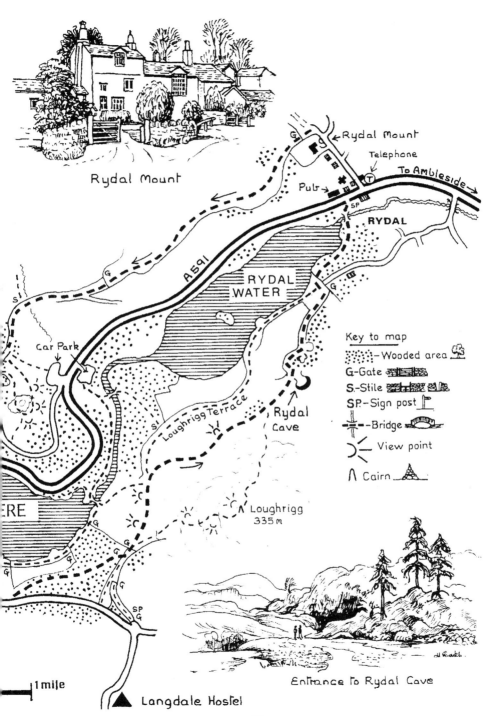

Rydal Mount

Rydal Mount

Telephone

To Ambleside

Pub

SP

RYDAL

A591

RYDAL
WATER

Car Park

Key to map

- Wooded area
G-Gate
S-Stile
SP-Sign post
-Bridge
View point
Cairn

Loughrigg Terrace

Rydal
Cave

Loughrigg
335 m

1 mile

Langdale Hostel

Entrance to Rydal Cave

45

Walks around Langdale YH and Grasmere YH

see page 42

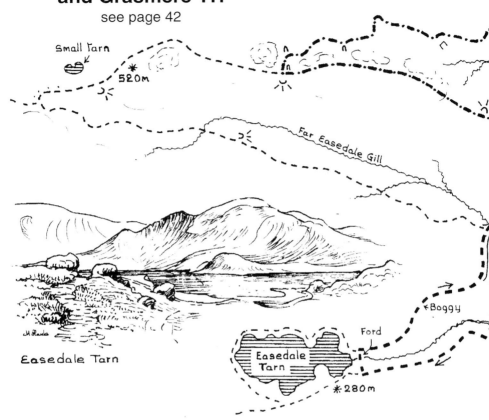

Small Tarn

520m

Far Easedale Gill

Easedale Tarn

Easedale Tarn

Boggy

Ford

280m

Easedale Tarn ▪ ▪ ▪

Easy walk about
4 miles 6½km in total
Takes between 2 & 3 hours.

Helm Crag. ▪ ▪ — ▪ — ▪ —

Hard climb to Helm Crag easy ridge
walk offering fine views.
Walk should only be made in good
weather. 7½miles - 12km in total
Takes between 4 & 5 hours.

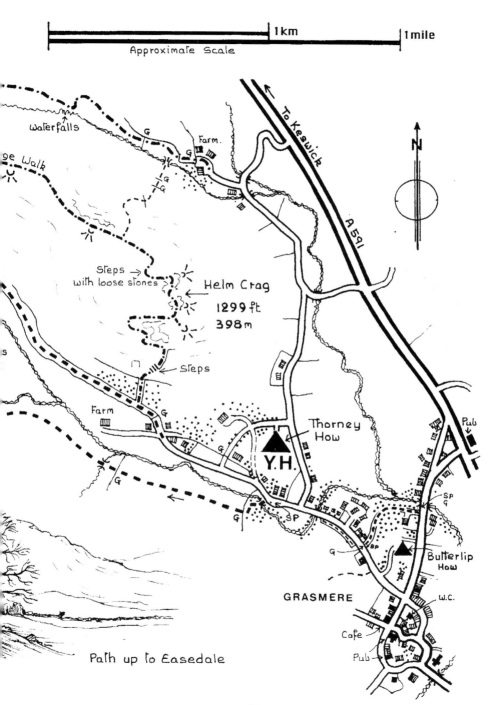

Approximate Scale

1km

1mile

Waterfalls

ge Walk

To Keswick

A 591

N

Farm.

Steps → with loose stones

Helm Crag
1299 ft
398 m

Steps

Farm

Thorney How

Y.H.

Pub

Butterlip How

GRASMERE

W.C.

Cafe

Pub

Path up to Easedale

47

Walking route between
Coniston YH and Hawkshead YH

see page 43

Distance by main route 6 miles. 9½ KM ━ ━ ━ ━
Shorter route through woods 5 miles. 8 KM ━ ━ ━
Add an extra 1 mile. 1·6 KM. from Coppermines Y.H.

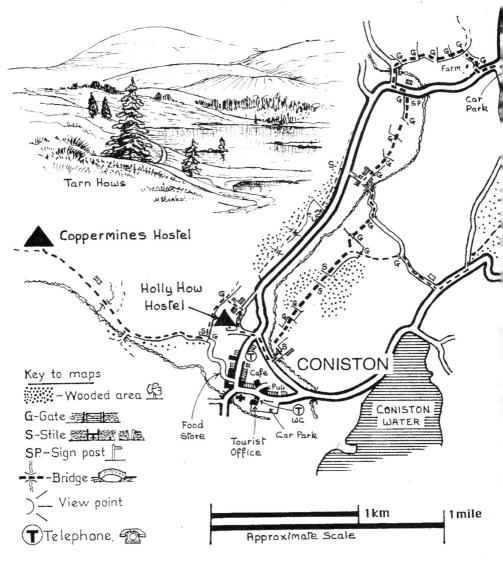

Tarn Hows

▲ Coppermines Hostel

Holly How
Hostel

CONISTON

CONISTON
WATER

Farm

Car
Park

Cafe

Pub

WC

Food
Store

Tourist
Office

Car Park

Key to maps
▓▓▓ — Wooded area 🌳
G - Gate
S.- Stile
SP— Sign post
━╪━ -Bridge
)—(View point
Ⓣ Telephone.

| 1km | | 1mile |

Approximate Scale

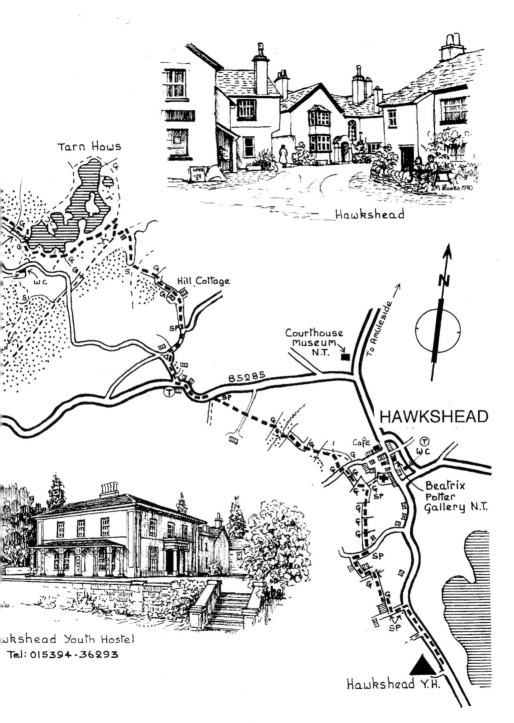

Tarn Hows

Hawkshead

Hill Cottage

Courthouse museum N.T.

To Ambleside

N

B5285

HAWKSHEAD

Cafe

WC

Beatrix Potter Gallery N.T.

Hawkshead Youth Hostel
Tel: 015394-36293

Hawkshead Y.H.

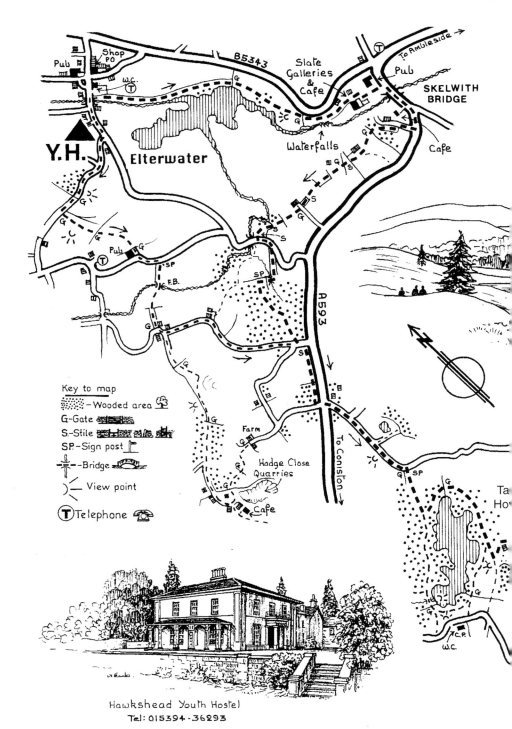

Pub
Shop PO
W.C.
T
B5343
Slate Galleries & Cafe
T
To Ambleside
Pub
SKELWITH BRIDGE
Y.H.
Elterwater
Waterfalls
Cafe
Pub
T
SP
F.B.
SP
A593
G

Key to map

- :::: – Wooded area
- G – Gate
- S. – Stile
- SP. – Sign post
- Bridge
-)(– View point
- T Telephone

Farm
Hodge Close Quarries
Cafe
To Coniston
SP
W.C.
Ta
Ho

Hawkshead Youth Hostel
Tel: 015394-36293

50

Walking route between Elterwater YH and Hawkshead YH

see page 43

Approximate distance by both routes 7.5 miles, 12 Km.

Tarn Hows

Hawkshead Village

Courthouse Museum N.T.

Beatrix Potter Gallery N.T.

W.C.

Hill Cottage

B5286

Cafe

Pub

Pub

HAWKSHEAD

ESTHWAITE WATER

Hawkshead Hill

1km   1mile

Approximate Scale

Y.H.

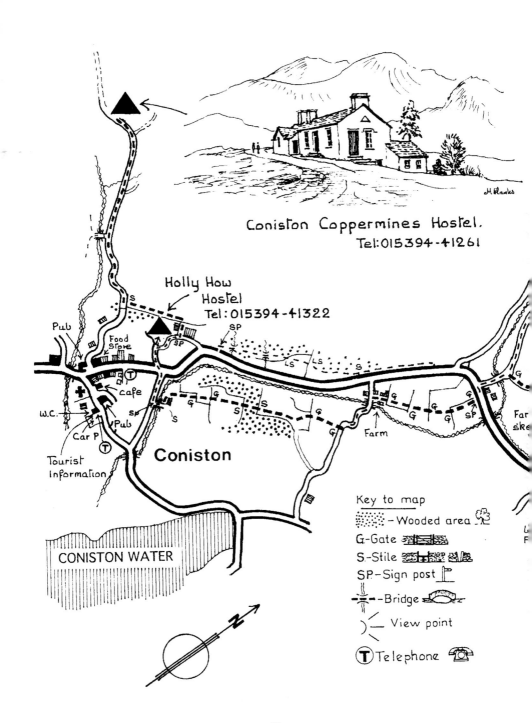

Coniston Coppermines Hostel.
Tel: 015394-41261

Holly How Hostel
Tel: 015394-41322

Pub

Food Store

SP

LS   LS   S

cafe

G   G   S   S   G   G   SP   Far
ske

W.C.

SP   S   Farm

Car P

Pub

Tourist Information

Coniston

CONISTON WATER

Key to map
⸭⸭⸭ – Wooded area 🌳
G-Gate
S-Stile
SP-Sign post
–⸬–-Bridge
)– View point
Ⓣ Telephone ☎

52

Walking route between Coniston YH and Ambleside YH: Map 1

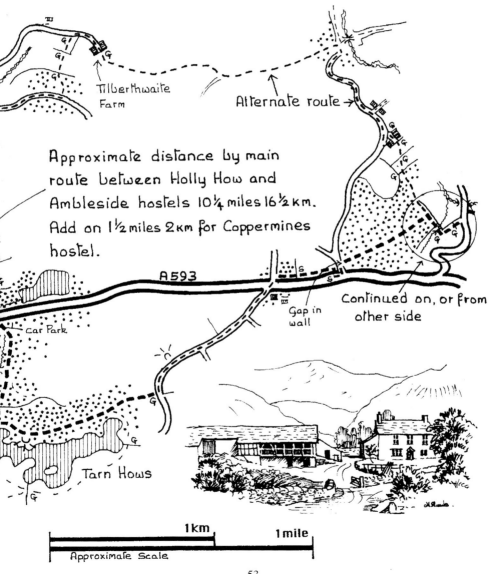

Tilberthwaite Farm

Alternate route →

Approximate distance by main route between Holly How and Ambleside hostels 10¼ miles 16½ km. Add on 1½ miles 2km for Coppermines hostel.

A593

Continued on, or from other side

Gap in wall

Car Park

Tarn Hows

1km

1mile

Approximate Scale

Coniston Holly How Youth Hostel
Tel: 015394_41323.

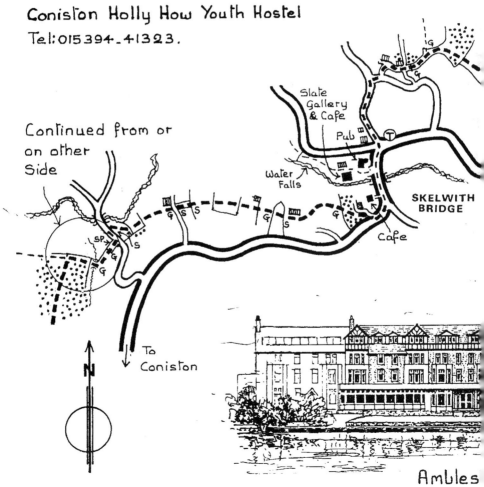

Continued from or
on other
Side

Slate
Gallery
& Cafe

Pub

Water
Falls

SKELWITH
BRIDGE

Cafe

To
Coniston

N

Ambles

Walking route between
Coniston YH and Ambleside YH: Map 2

see page 43

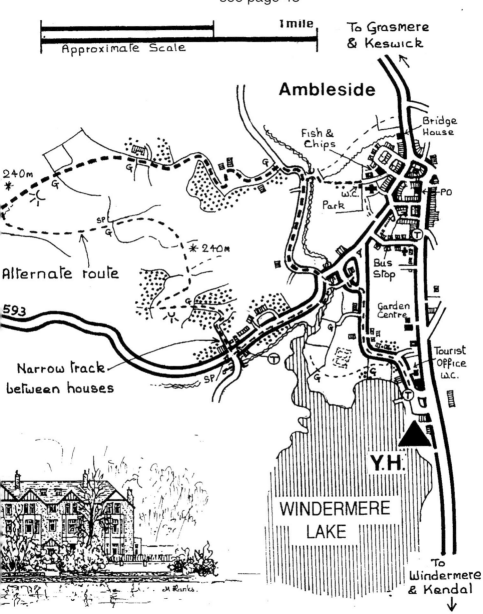

1 mile

Approximate Scale

To Grasmere & Keswick

Ambleside

Fish & Chips

Bridge House

240m

SP

240m

Alternate route

593

Narrow track between houses

SP

W.C.
Park

PO

Bus Stop

Garden Centre

T

Tourist Office
W.C.

Y.H.

WINDERMERE
LAKE

To Windermere & Kendal

M Ranks.

Hostel Tel: 015394-32304

Coniston YH to Eskdale YH
(The maps are on pages 58/61)

This route follows the Walna Scar Road, now a track, over the Seathwaite Fells to Dunnerdale and on below Harter Fell to Eskdale. Follow Church Beck, as though heading for Coniston Copper Mines YH and cross the Miner's Bridge. Skirt around the fell to reach Walna Scar Road. The track is easy to follow across the fells, eventually dropping down Long House Gill to cross the fields over the Tarn Beck. A little further on, the River Duddon is crossed by stepping stones. If the river is high this may be impassable, causing a detour via Seathwaite (see map).

Beyond the River Duddon the path rises up Grassguards Gill below Harter Fell before dropping down into Eskdale to the west of Birker Fell. On descending into Eskdale, Penny Hill Farm and Doctor Bridge are passed to reach Eskdale YH.

Low level walks from Coniston YH
(The maps are on pages 62/65)

From Martyn's map you will see various short circular walks around Church Beck and also using the Walna Scar Road track. A longer route follows the track before heading via the former Homestead Quarry down Torver Beck to Torver village. From here the route heads for Coniston Water and Torver Common Wood. The path returns to Coniston along the lakeside and past Coniston Hall. Look out for the restored steam driven launch *Gondola* on the lake. It is owned by the National Trust and can be booked at the Coniston jetty. Here Donald Campbell was based for his attempts to break the water speed record.

There are a variety of paths north of Coniston, most of which have been used by Martyn in his inter-hostel routes mentioned above. An additional path is through the disused Hodge Close quarries, now with a large lake in the middle. This is a pleasant undulating path, clearly defined and easily linked with other routes marked on the map. It can be accessed from Tilberthwaite or Stang End, near Slater Bridge. Notice also the path between Hodge Close Quarry and Yew Tree Farm via Holme Fell which drops down into the wood above Yew Tree Tarn.

Walks from Eskdale YH
(The map is on pages 66/67)

Walk past the Woolpack Inn and cross the River Esk at Doctor Bridge. The path runs up the far side of Eskdale from the youth hostel. It leaves the valley where the road starts to climb up to the Hard Knott Pass. This brings you to the remains of Hard Knott Roman Fort, now in the care of English Heritage. It is a wonderful place to visit and to try and envisage what life was like here nearly 2,000 years ago.

The path returns to the valley and turns right to cross the river just beyond Brotherilkeld Farm. Beyond the footbridge is Taw House and a level path which leads down to the road near to the youth hostel.

Eskdale YH to Wast Water YH

(The maps are on pages 68/71)

The River Esk is followed down to Eskdale Green. The valley is flat and your apprecia-
tion of the scenery can be enhanced by the diminutive steam trains on the Ravenglass and
Eskdale Railway. In fact the route crosses the railway line by The Green Station. The path
leaves the road north of the station by the bank and shop. It quickly drops into Miterdale,
a lovely and little known valley.

Miterdale Forest is then crossed to Ireton Fell where the path descends to Wasdale with
superb views up Wast Water. The path turns towards the lake at a signpost and descends
through Easthwaite Farm to follow the lake to Wast Water YH.

Eskdale YH to Ravensglass

(The maps are on pages 68/69 and 72/73)

On leaving the hostel turn right and having passed the Woolpack Inn turn left to Doctor
Bridge. From here a path heads through river-meadows to Boot Church. There are stepping stones here which should be crossed. If the river is high, cross Doctor Bridge and
walk down the other side of the river via Low Birker Farm. Below Boot Church the path
passes through woodland close to the River Esk before fields are crossed to reach the
Eskdale Green to Ulpha road.

Turn right past the pub to Eskdale Green Station, then turn left before the station
leading up onto Muncaster Fell. This is not too high, rising to 758ft (231m). As a result,
this walk is often available when the clouds drop to low levels and preclude access to the
high fells. There are good views to the sea from the fell. Look out for a couple of boggy
areas enroute. This is not a long fell and you are soon descending towards Ravensglass.

On reaching the A595, turn left and then right to pass Muncaster Castle, reaching
Ravensglass after passing the remains of a Roman bath house. There is a pub and a couple
of cafés in the village, plus the prospect of a steam hauled train for the return journey to
Dalegarth Station. This is just over 1 mile from the youth hostel. Take your membership
card with you to get a reduction on the train fare.

Walking route between
Coniston YH and Eskdale YH: Map 1

see page 56

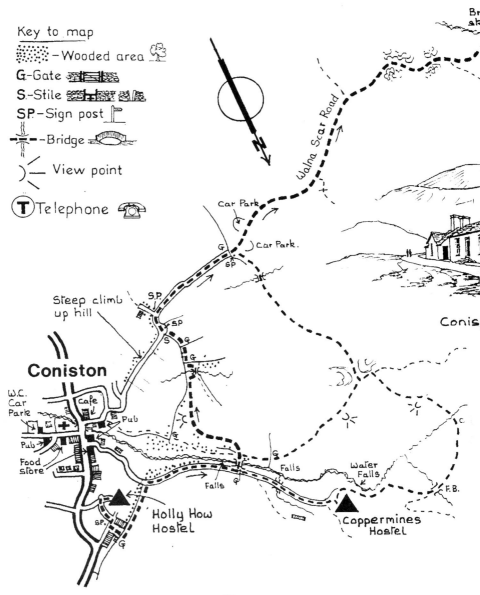

Key to map

▦ – Wooded area

G. – Gate

S. – Stile

S.P. – Sign post

✚ – Bridge

)⌣ View point

Ⓣ Telephone

Car Park

Walna Scar Road

Car Park.

Steep climb up hill

S.P.

S.P.

G

S

G

Coniston

Conis

W.C.
Car
Park

Cafe

Pub

Pub →

Food store

Falls

Water Falls

Falls

F.B.

C.

Holly How Hostel

Coppermines Hostel

S.P.

Br
ak

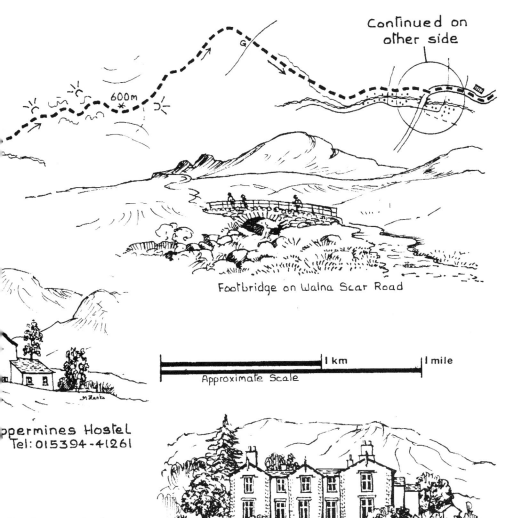

Continued on other side

600m

Footbridge on Walna Scar Road

1 km   1 mile

Approximate Scale

ppermines Hostel
Tel: 015394-41261

Coniston Holly How Hostel Tel: 015394-41323

Distance between
Coniston & Eskdale
by direct route-over
stepping stones
11 miles -17½ k.m.
Alternative wet weather
route via Seathwaite
12¾ miles - 20 k.m.

Allow about 7 hours for direct
route - 8 hours for alternative route

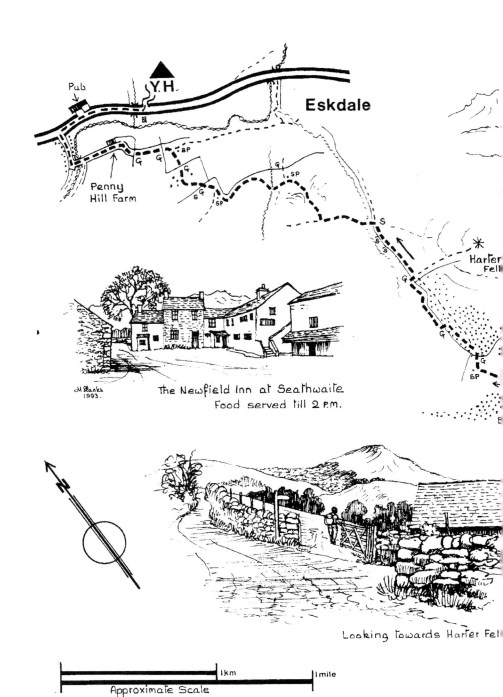

Pub

Y.H.

Eskdale

Penny
Hill Farm

Harter
Fell

The Newfield Inn at Seathwaite
Food served till 2 p.m.

M Planks
1993.

N

Looking towards Harter Fell

1km   1mile

Approximate Scale

Walking route between Coniston YH and Eskdale YH: Map 2

see page 56

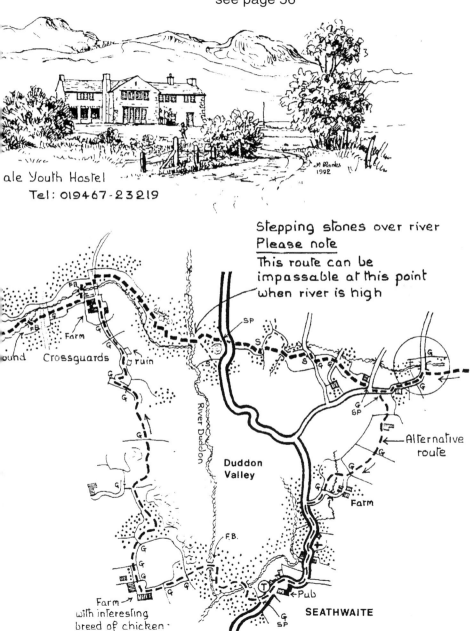

ale Youth Hostel

Tel: 019467-23219

Stepping stones over river

Please note

This route can be impassable at this point when river is high

SP

S

S

G

G

G

Farm

ound   Crossguards   ruin

G

G

G

River Duddon

Duddon Valley

G

SP

G

Alternative route

G

G

G

Farm

F.B.

G

Farm →
with interesting
breed of chicken·

G

G

G

G

T

← Pub

SEATHWAITE

G
SP

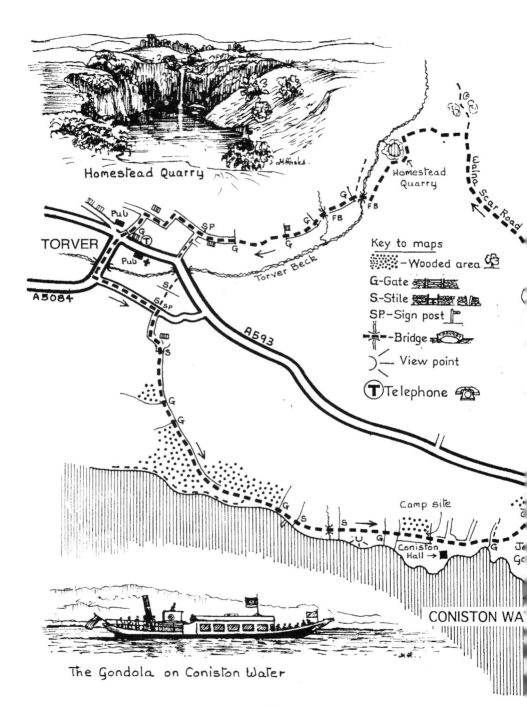

Homestead Quarry

Homestead Quarry

Elmo Scar Road

TORVER

Pub

Pub

A5084

Torver Beck

A593

Key to maps

▓▓ —Wooded area

G—Gate

S—Stile

SP—Sign post

—Bridge

)— View point

(T) Telephone

Camp site

Coniston Hall →

CONISTON WA

The Gondola on Coniston Water

Low level Walks from Coniston YH

see page 56

Approximate distance of main circular walk 9½ miles 15 Km and takes about 6½ hours.

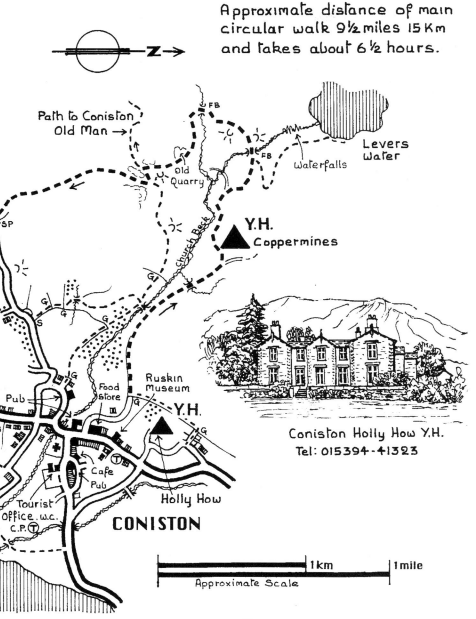

Path to Coniston Old Man →

Levers Water

Waterfalls

Old Quarry

Church Beck

Y.H.
Coppermines

Ruskin Museum

Food Store

Pub

Cafe
Pub

Tourist Office. w.c.
C.P.

Holly How

Y.H.

CONISTON

Coniston Holly How Y.H.
Tel: 015394-41323

1 km   1 mile
Approximate Scale

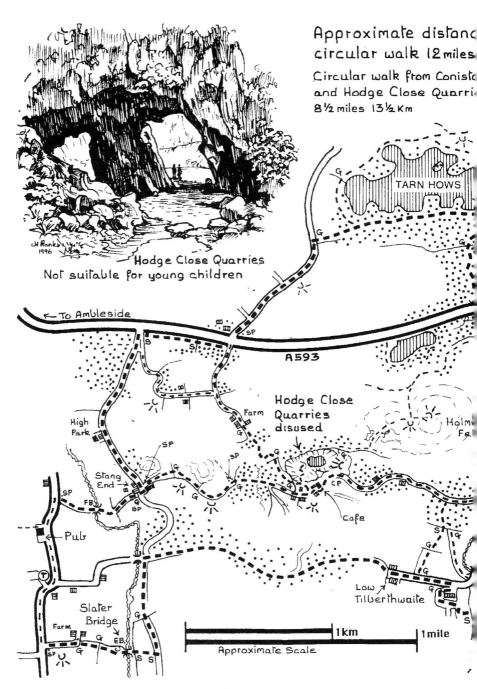

Approximate distanc
circular walk 12 miles

Circular walk from Conista
and Hodge Close Quarri
8½ miles 13½ Km

Hodge Close Quarries
Not suitable for young children

Low level Walks from Coniston YH

see page 56

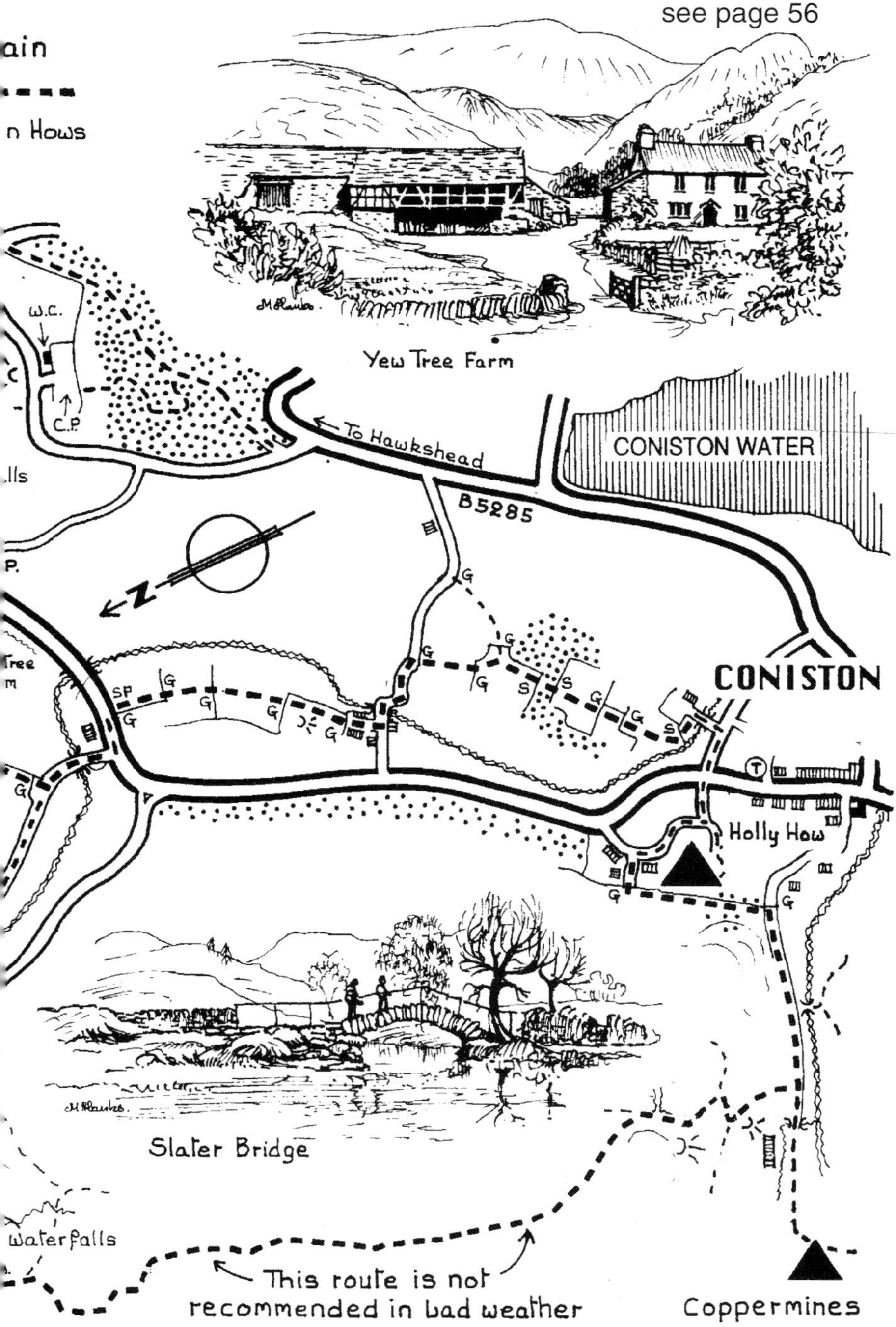
ain
n Hows
W.C.
C.P.
lls
P.
Yew Tree Farm
To Hawkshead
B5285
CONISTON WATER
N
CONISTON
SP
G
S
T
Holly How
Slater Bridge
waterfalls
This route is not recommended in bad weather
Coppermines

Brotherilkeld Farm.

Key to maps

- Wooded area
- G-Gate
- S-Stile
- SP-Sign post
- Bridge
- View point
- T Telephone.

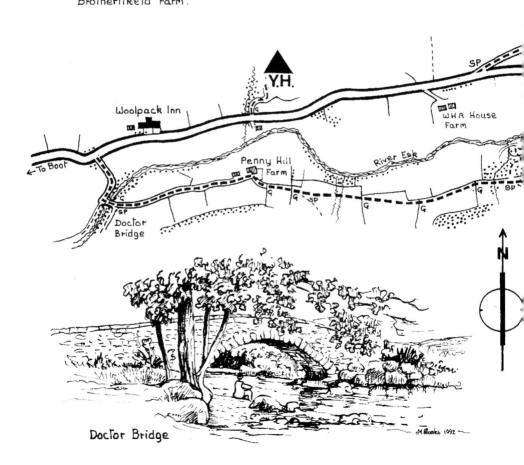

Doctor Bridge

Walks around Eskdale YH

see page 56

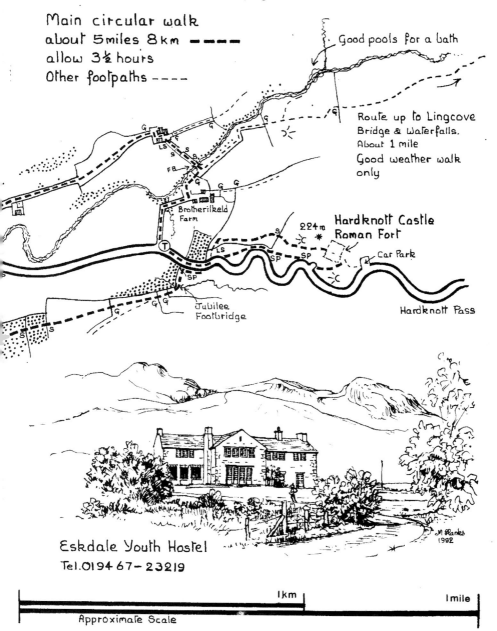

Main circular walk
about 5miles 8km ━ ━ ━
allow 3½ hours
Other footpaths ─ ─ ─ ─

Good pools for a bath

Route up to Lingcove
Bridge & Waterfalls.
About 1 mile
Good weather walk
only

Brotherilkeld Farm

Hardknott Castle
Roman Fort

224m

Car Park

Hardknott Pass

Jubilee Footbridge

Eskdale Youth Hostel
Tel.019467-23219

1km   1mile
Approximate Scale

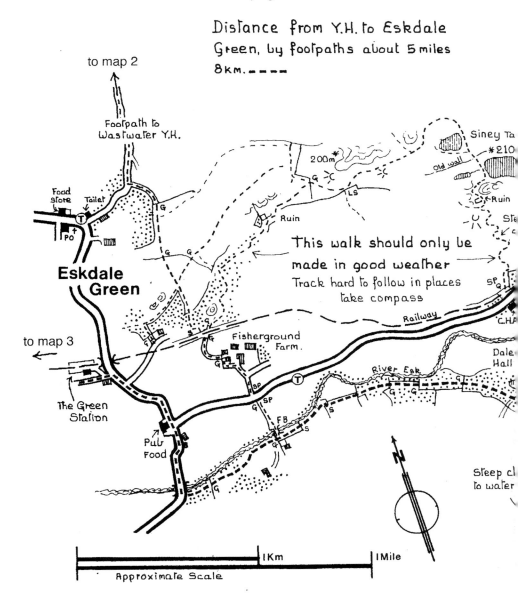

Distance from Y.H. to Eskdale Green, by footpaths about 5 miles 8km. - - - -

to map 2

Footpath to Wastwater Y.H.

Food store

Toilet

PO

Eskdale Green

to map 3

The Green Station

Pub Food

200m

Ruin

Old wall

Siney Ta

#210

Ruin

St

This walk should only be made in good weather
Track hard to follow in places
take compass

Railway

C.H.

Fisherground Farm.

River Esk

Dale Hall

SP

FB

Steep cl to water

N

1 Km

1 Mile

Approximate Scale

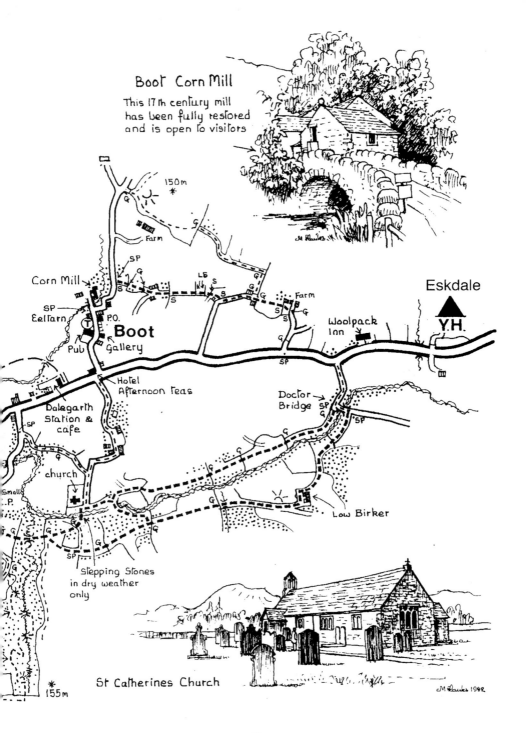

Boot Corn Mill

This 17th century mill
has been fully restored
and is open to visitors

150m

Farm

SP

Corn Mill

SP
Eeltarn

Boot

Pub   Gallery

Hotel
Afternoon Teas

Dalegarth
Station &
cafe

church

Small
P.

Stepping Stones
in dry weather
only

155m

LS
S

Farm

Woolpack
Inn

Eskdale

Y.H.

Doctor
Bridge   SP

SP

Low Birker

St Catherines Church

Walk from EskdaleYH to Wast Water YH:Map 2

see page 57

Approximate time
3 to 3½ hours steady walk

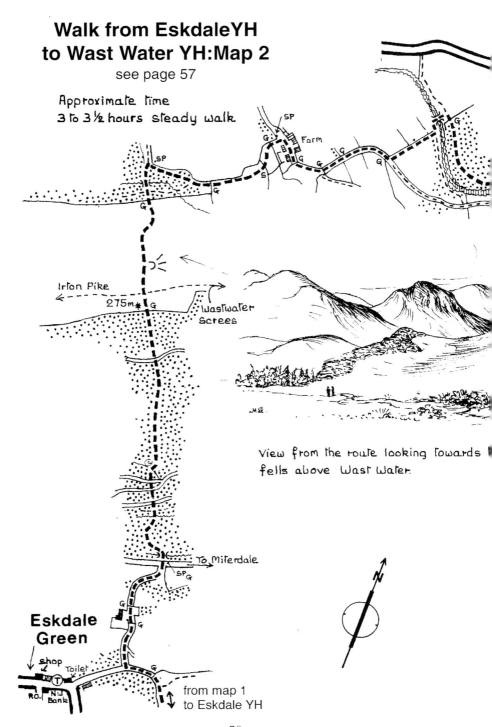

Irton Pike

275m *

Wastwater Screes

Farm

View from the route looking towards fells above Wast Water.

To Miterdale

Eskdale Green

Shop

Toilet

Rd. NW Bank

from map 1
to Eskdale YH

Distance between Eskdale
Green and Wastwater Y.H.
$3\frac{3}{4}$ miles 6 km
Total distance by footpath
between the two hostels
about $8\frac{3}{4}$ miles 14 km.

Y.H.

WAST WATER

Wastwater Youth Hostel Tel: 019467-26222

Eskdale Youth Hostel
Tel. 019467-23219

1km   1mile

Approximate scale

Walk from EskdaleYH to Ravenglass Map 3

see page 57

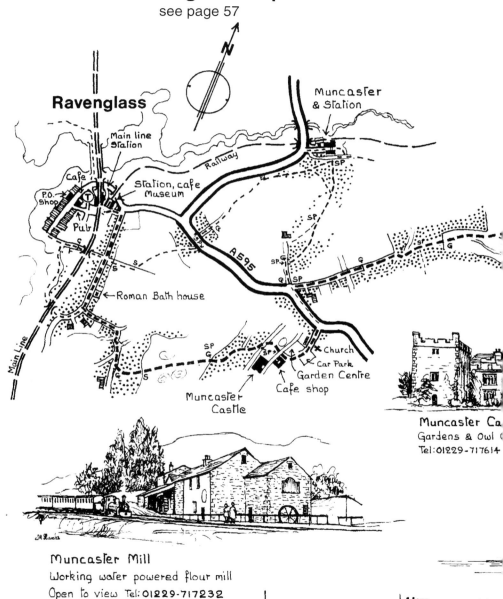

N

Ravenglass

Muncaster & Station

Main line Station

Railway

Café

Station, café Museum

P.O. Shop

T

Pub

A595

SP

SP

SP

G

G

G

SP

SP

←Roman Bath house

Main Line

SP
G

SP

× Church

Car Park

Garden Centre

Café shop

Muncaster Castle

S
G

Muncaster Ca
Gardens & Owl
Tel:01229-717614

Muncaster Mill
Working water powered flour mill
Open to view Tel:01229-717232

1km

1m

Approximate Scale

Ravenglass & Eskdale Railway

This attractive narrow gauge railway runs a regular service throughout the year. Check with warden for latest time table. Reductions for YHA members with cards.
Tel: 0229-717171

Distance by footpath from Green Station to Ravenglass 7miles-11km.
This is a good moorland walk offering fine views.

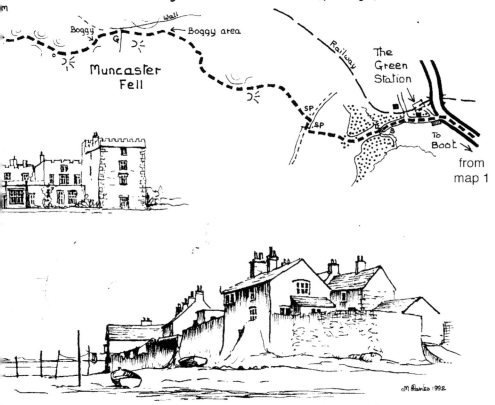

Picturesque village of Ravenglass

73

Low level walks around Wast Water YH

(The maps are on pages 76/79)

A flat 10 mile (16km) walk up the far side of the lake from the YH to Wasdale Head is very pleasant. The village lies before a backdrop of Great Gable, Scafell Pike, Kirk Fell and Yewbarrow. The lake is unusual, as it is owned by the National Trust. The screes which dominate the side of Ilgill Head can be tricky in wet weather or for young children. The return route is down the lane which runs all the way back to the hostel.

An alternative route runs down to Santon Bridge. From the end of the lake, the path goes down to Nether Wasdale. Here it follows the Santon Bridge road before skirting Latterbarrow and Irton Pike, passing through forested areas to reach the River Irt at Santon Bridge. The path then follows the river valley back to Nether Wasdale. Note the picnic spot recommended by Martyn!

Black Sail Hut YH to Honister Hause YH

(The map is on pages 80/81)

Black Sail Hut YH is situated in a first class situation for fell walkers. Since the distance shown on the map to Honister Hause is not far, 3.25 miles (5km), you may wish to deviate a little to suit your preference. The route goes past the back of the hostel and climbs up the gully below Seavy Knott. The path then crosses the fell to join the old quarry tramway which leads directly down to Honister Hause.

An alternative route is to head from Black Sail towards Ennerdale Forest and climb up to the right heading for Scarth Gap. Turn right here and climb up the ridge path onto The Haystacks, passing Innominate and Blackbeck Tarns. This route drops down to Honister to the north of the tramway. It is suitable for more seasoned walkers, and the views on a clear day are magnificent!

Ennerdale YH to Black Sail Hut YH

(The map is on pages 82/83)

You have a choice here of either side of the valley until the memorial bridge is reached and the two paths come together. The one on the far side of the beck from the hostel climbs higher up the hillside, so it's up to you!

Eventually Ennerdale Forest is left behind and Black Sail can be seen ahead, almost lost against the backcloth of the fells including Great Gable and Brandreth. In fact Ennerdale is surrounded by high fells, with Pillar to the south and the peaks of Red Pike, High Stile, High Crag and Haystacks to the north.

Walks from Ennerdale YH

(The map is on pages 84/85)

An 8 miles (12.8km) circular path around Ennerdale Water makes a lovely walk, especially if a detour is made to Ennerdale Bridge. Here for your lunchtime break is a choice of two pubs. The lake path keeps fairly close to the water for the whole distance.

Cockermouth YH to Ennerdale YH

(The maps are on pages 86/89)

This is a long route of 16.5 miles (26.5km). It follows the River Cocker out of Cockermouth, heading south to Loweswater. Much of this section is on country lanes, running to the village of Mosser. Beyond there the lane is unsurfaced, dropping steeply down to the lake and Loweswater village. From here the route goes south once more down Mosedale, between Loweswater Fell and Mellbreak. At the top end of the dale, the route crosses a gap in the fells to reach Ennerdale Water.

Here the path runs along the lakeside below Ennerdale Forest to reach the hostel about one mile beyond the end of the lake.

YOUTH HOSTELLER'S WALKING GUIDES

Forthcoming Titles in this Series:

– Yorkshire Dales and Moors

– The Peak District

These two new titles will be available shortly. Please send or telephone for details, and let us know if you have any particular wish for a similar book in further areas of the UK.

LANDMARK
Publishing Ltd ● ● ● ●

Waterloo House, 12 Compton, Ashbourne, Derbyshire DE6 1DA England

---

Low level Walks from Wast Water YH

see page 74

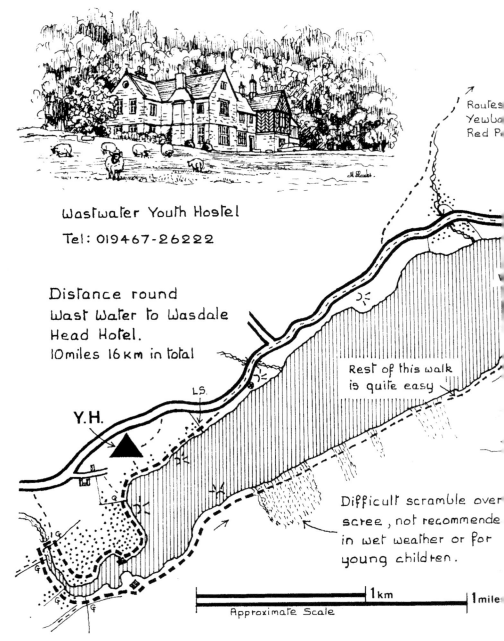

Wastwater Youth Hostel

Tel: 019467-26222

Distance round
Wast Water to Wasdale
Head Hotel.
10 miles 16 km in total

Routes
Yewba
Red P

Rest of this walk
is quite easy

Y.H.

L.S.

Difficult scramble over
scree, not recommende
in wet weather or for
young children.

|————————————| 1 km | 1 mile

Approximate Scale

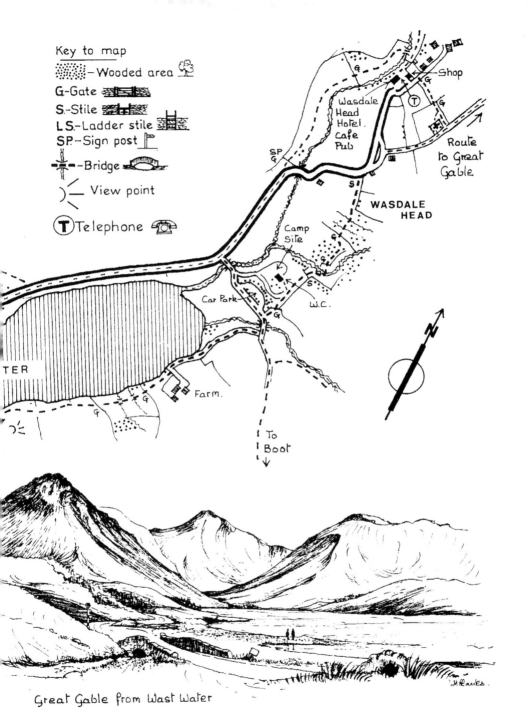

Key to map
░░ – Wooded area
G – Gate
S. – Stile
L S. – Ladder stile
SP. – Sign post
✦ – Bridge
)‿ – View point
(T) Telephone

Shop
Wasdale Head Hotel Cafe Pub
Route to Great Gable
WASDALE HEAD
Camp Site
Car Park
W.C.
TER
Farm.
To Boot

Great Gable from Wast Water

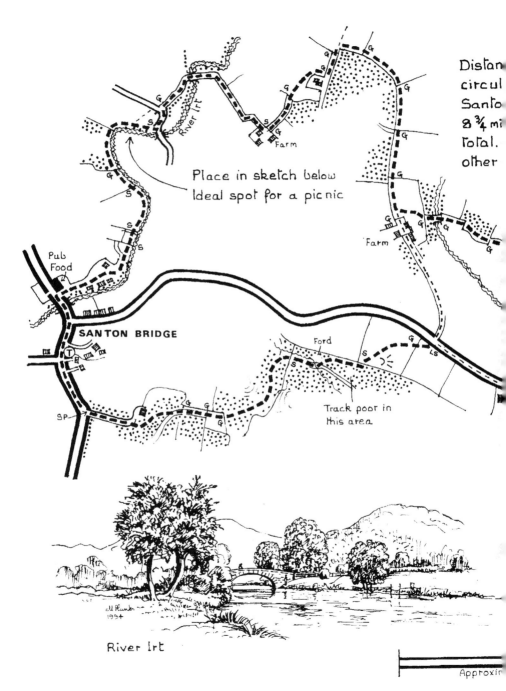

Distan
circul
Santo
8 ¾ mi
Total.
other

River Irt

Place in sketch below
Ideal spot for a picnic

Farm

Farm

Pub
Food

SANTON BRIDGE

Ford

Track poor in
this area

River Irt

Approxir

Low level Walks from Wast Water YH

see page 74

The two pubs at Nether Wasdale

WAST WATER

1 km
1 mile

View looking back down Ennerdale.

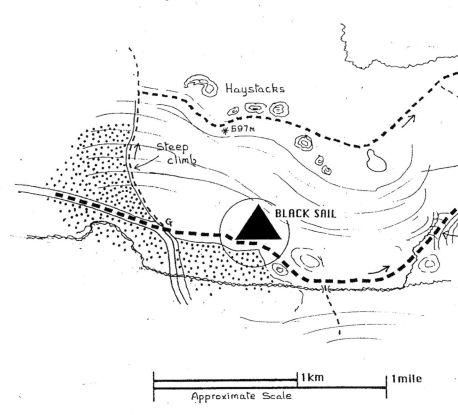

Haystacks

*597m

steep climb

G

BLACK SAIL

1km | 1mile

Approximate Scale

Walking route between
Black Sail YH and Honister Hause YH

see page 74

Distance by main route 3¼ miles 5 km.

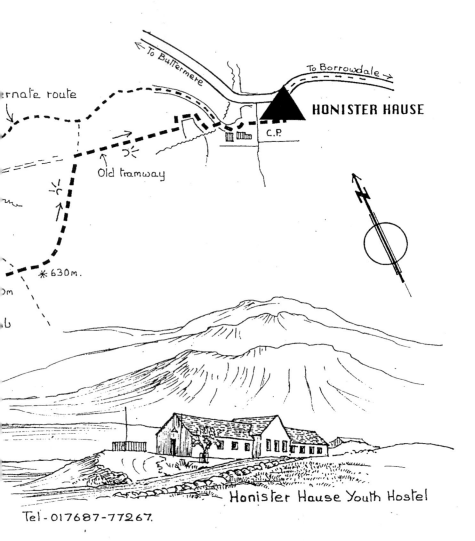

To Buttermere

To Borrowdale →

ernate route

HONISTER HAUSE

C.P.

Old tramway

✳ 630m.

Honister Hause Youth Hostel

Tel - 017687 - 77267.

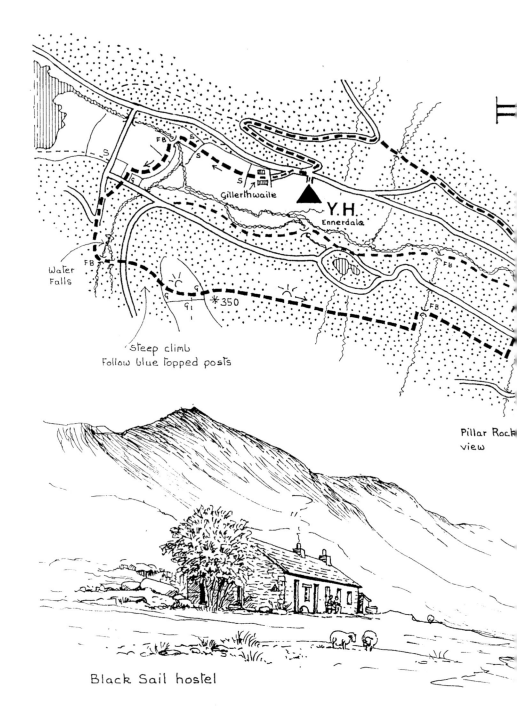

FB

S

Gillerthwaite

Y.H.
Ennerdale

Water
Falls

FB

FB

FB

✳350

Steep climb
Follow blue topped posts

Pillar Rock
view

Black Sail hostel

Walking route between
Ennerdale YH and Black Sail YH

see page 74

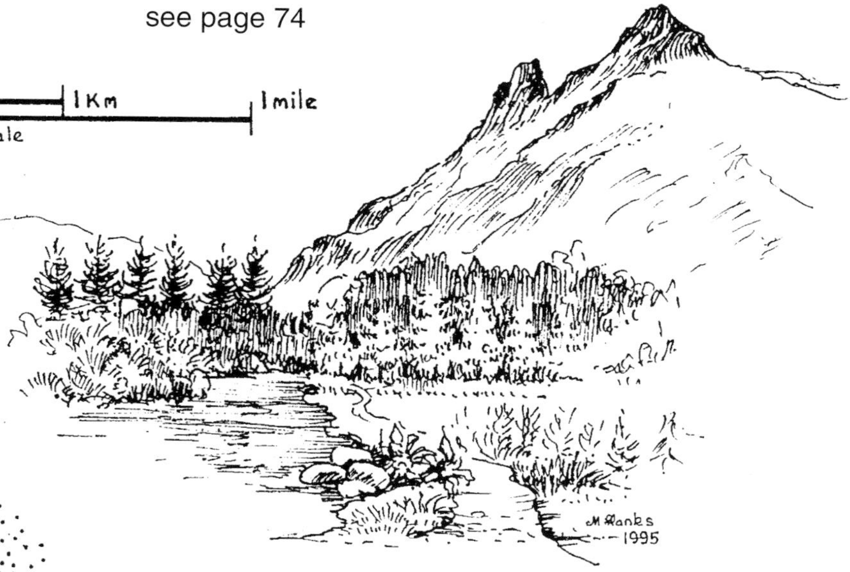

1 Km   1 mile

ximate Scale

M. Ranks
1995

Pillar Rock from the track

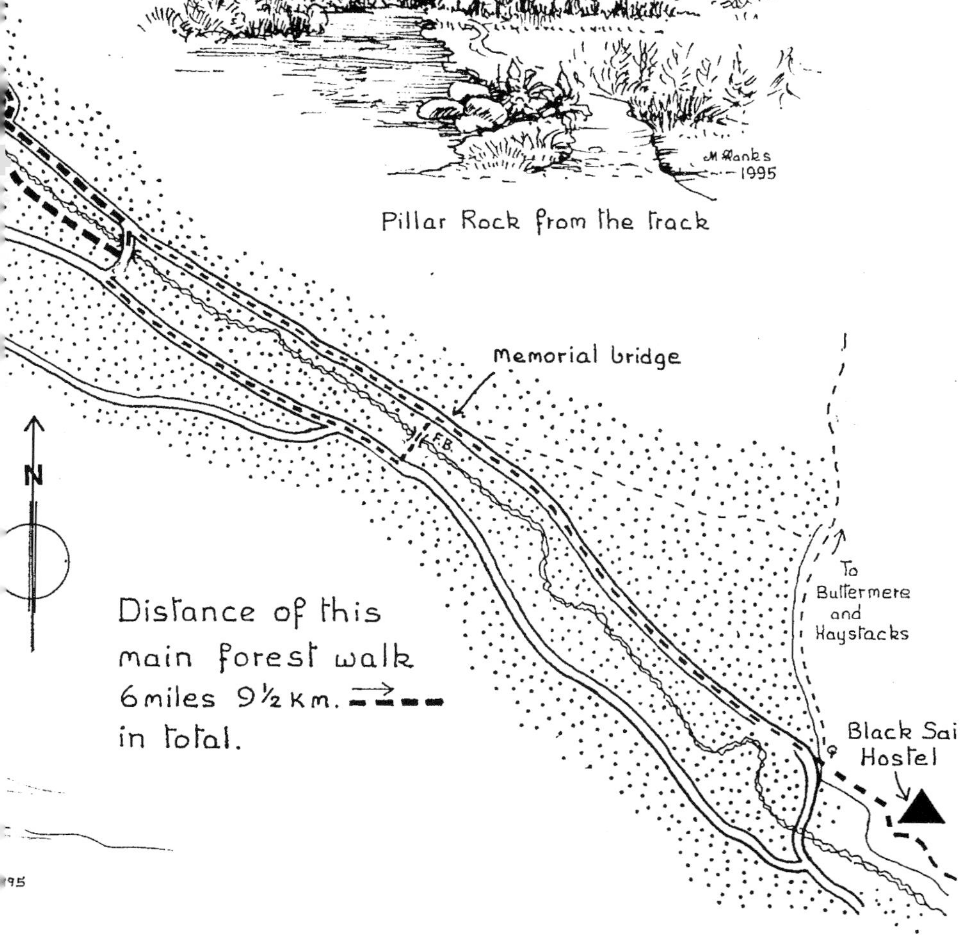

memorial bridge

F.B.

N

To
Buttermere
and
Haystacks

Distance of this
main forest walk
6 miles 9½ km.
in total.

Black Sail
Hostel

Distance round lake from hostel 8miles 12½km in total
Add on an extra 2½miles 4km for Ennerdale Bridge

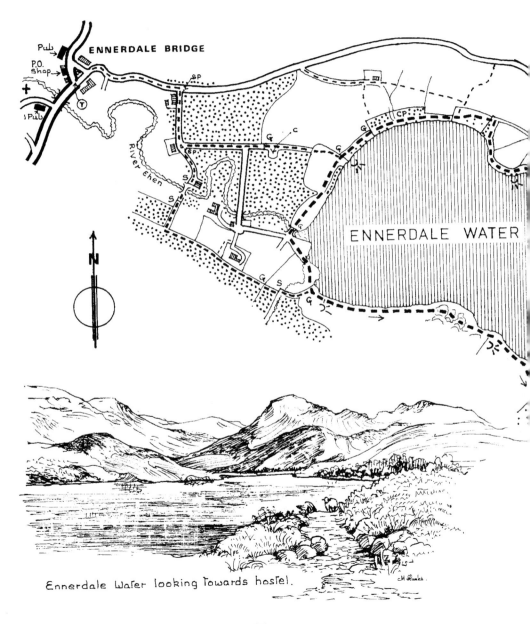

Ennerdale Water looking towards hostel.

Walks from Ennerdale YH

see page 75

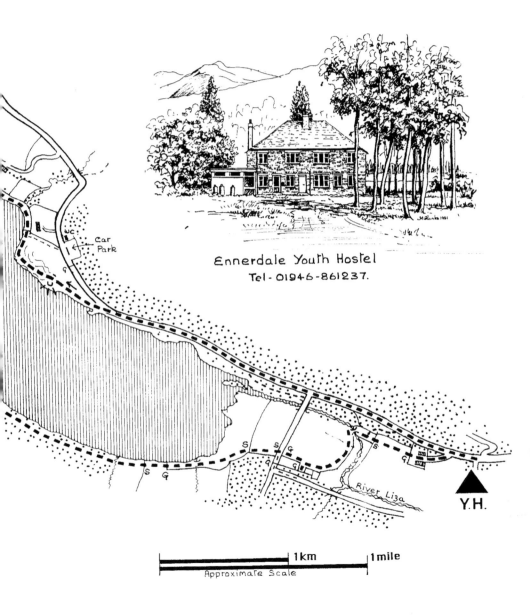

Ennerdale Youth Hostel
Tel - 01946-861237.

Car Park

River Liza

Y.H.

1km | 1mile
Approximate Scale

85

Walking route between
Cockermouth YH and Ennerdale YH: Map 1
see page 75

Approximate distance 16.5 miles, 26.5 Km

Key to maps

- 𝌆 -Wooded area
- G-Gate
- S.-Stile
- SP.-Sign post
- -Bridge
-)— View point
- Ⓣ Telephone

This is a long but rewarding walk with some fine scenery, especially in the middle part where one can really get the feeling you are getting away from it all.

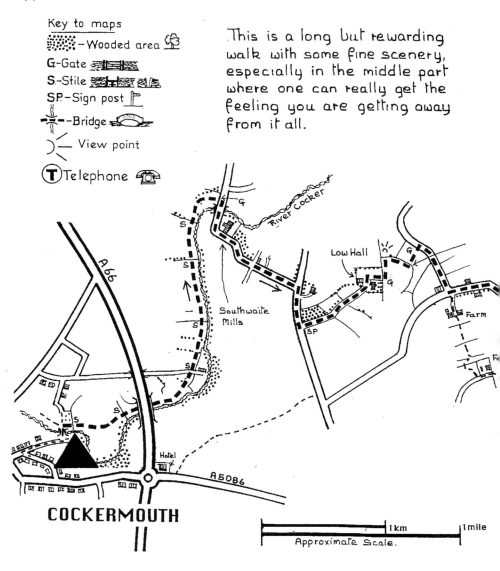

1 km   1 mile
Approximate Scale.

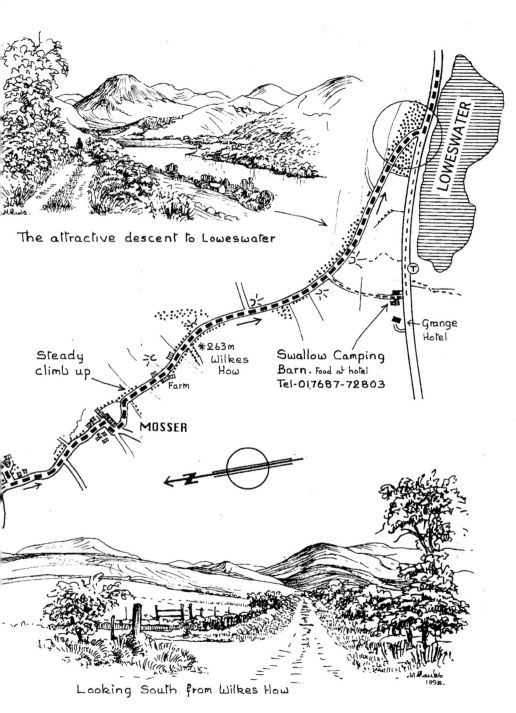

The attractive descent to Loweswater

LOWESWATER

Steady climb up

*263m
Wilkes
How

Farm

MOSSER

Swallow Camping
Barn. Food at hotel
Tel-017687-72803

Grange
Hotel

Looking South from Wilkes How

Walking route between Cockermouth YH and Ennerdale YH: Map 2

see page 75

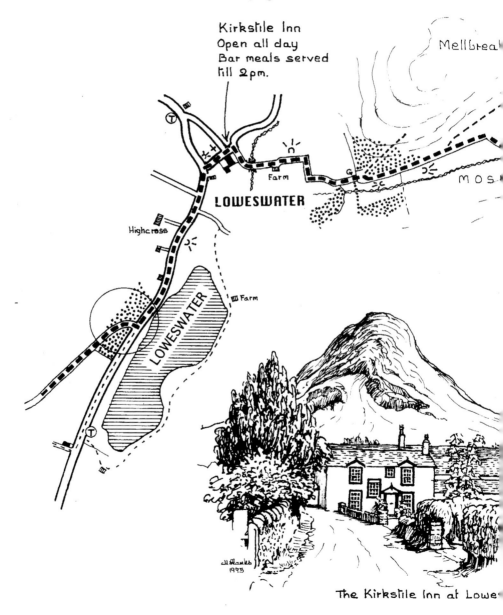

Kirkstile Inn
Open all day
Bar meals served
till 2pm.

Mellbrea

Farm

LOWESWATER

MOS

Highcross

LOWESWATER

Farm

cll Planks
1995

The Kirkstile Inn at Lowe

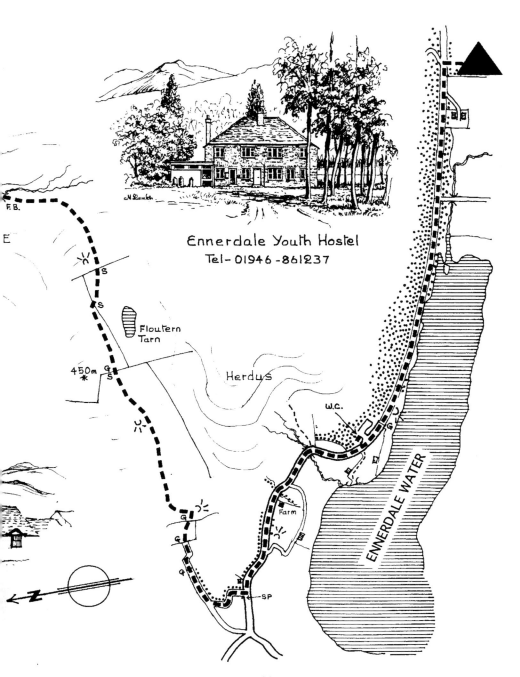

Ennerdale Youth Hostel
Tel- 01946 -861237

F.B.

E

S

S

Floutern
Tarn

450m

G
S

Herdus

W.C.

G

ENNERDALE WATER

Farm

G

G

G

SP

Cockermouth YH to Skiddaw House YH
(The maps are on pages 92/95)

This is another long walk of 15 miles (24km). It runs up the Derwent Valley to Isell Bridge where the River Derwent is crossed. The path continues across the fields to join a lane to reach Bassenthwaite village. It then cuts through more fields to climb the north flank of Skiddaw. Look for the signpost by Peter House Farm to the east of Bassenthwaite. Here the climb up onto the fells begins. The route gradually turns south to reach Skiddaw House, sheltered by trees and the mass of Skiddaw behind it.

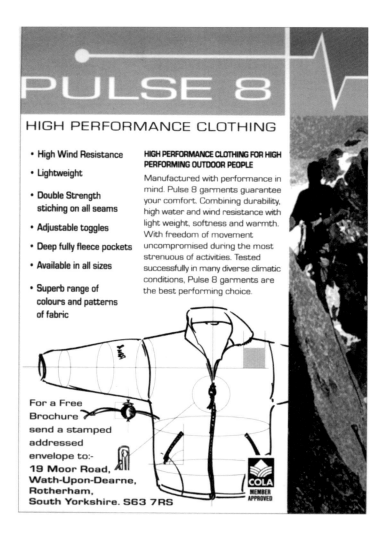

Keswick YH to Carrock Fell YH

(The map is on pages 96/97)

The low level route, which is recommended in bad weather, follows the former railway line to Threlkeld. It is reached conveniently by crossing the river in Station Road, adjacent to the youth hostel. From Threlkeld, the path skirts the foot of Blencathra to the hamlet of Scales. Here you have a choice of following a track to High Beckside or of following the River Glenderamackin to Mungrisdale.

On leaving Scales the path to the latter heads for a disused mine (which should be avoided). Ensure you bear to the right before reaching the mine to pick up the path in Mousthwaite Comb, or follow the dotted route on the map which starts by the pub.

High Beckside is just to the south of Mungrisdale, where the road goes to Mosedale and after a further two miles reaches Carrock Fell YH.

Keswick YH to Skiddaw House YH and Carrock Fell YH

(The map is on pages 98/99)

From Keswick YH cross the River Greta, the old railway and the A66 Keswick bypass. The route follows the Cumbria Way, climbs around the side of Lonscale Fell and follows the valley of the wonderfully named Glenderaterra Beck to reach Skiddaw House YH in about 4.25 hours.

From here the route proceeds towards the River Caldew and Carrock Fell, joining an old mine track which leads down to Mosedale where the road may be followed to Carrock Fell YH. This route should only be attempted in good weather. It is wise to advise the warden that you are using this route if a booking at Skiddaw House YH commits you to this way in poor weather conditions.

Carrock Fell YH to Skiddaw House YH

(The map is on pages 100/101)

The way via Mosedale is the reverse of the previous route but there is another alternative around the north side of Carrock Fell, including a path to the top of the fell. However, it is not recommended in bad weather. The path runs past Carrock Mine which was worked for lead and tungsten. The workings of these and other Lakeland mines should be avoided.

Walking route between
Cockermouth YH and Skiddaw House YH: Map 1
see page 90

Approximate distance 15 miles, 24 Km.

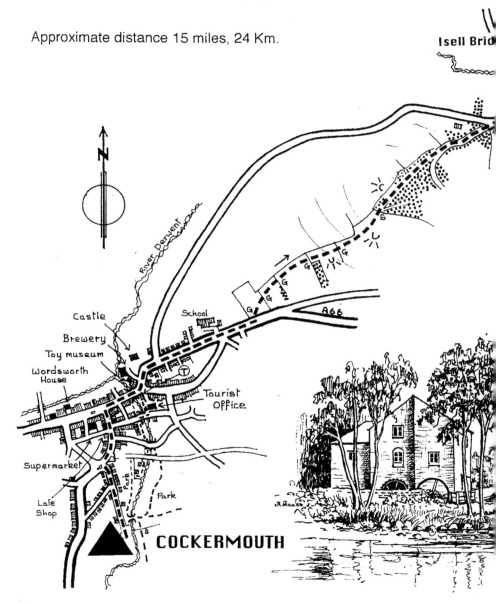

Isell Brid

Castle

Brewery

Toy museum

Wordsworth House

Supermarket

Lake Shop

School

Tourist Office

Park

A66

River Derwent

COCKERMOUTH

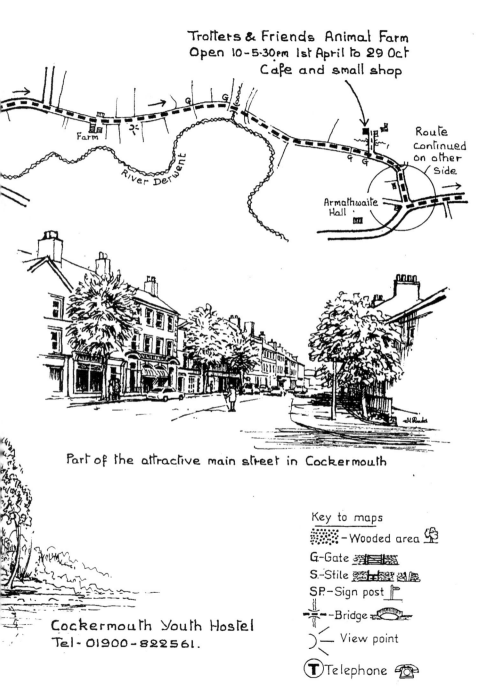

Trotters & Friends Animal Farm
Open 10-5.30pm 1st April to 29 Oct
Cafe and small shop

Farm

River Derwent

Route continued on other side

Armathwaite Hall

Part of the attractive main street in Cockermouth

Cockermouth Youth Hostel
Tel - 01900 - 822561.

Key to maps
▓▓▓ - Wooded area
G - Gate
S. - Stile
SP. - Sign post
-▪- - Bridge
)(- View point
(T) Telephone

Walking route between
Cockermouth YH and Skiddaw House YH: Map 2

see page 90

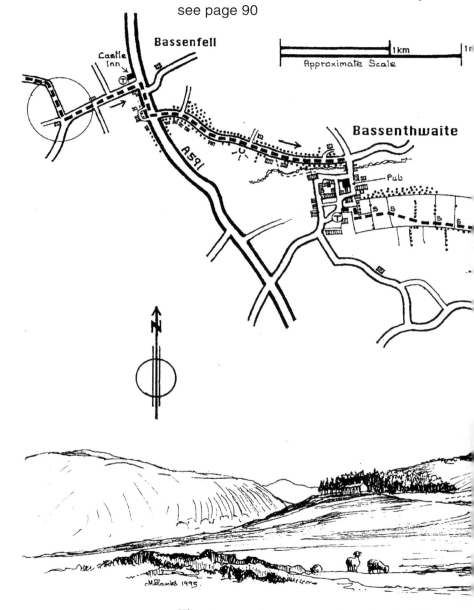

The impressive panoramic view looking at the hostel from the track.

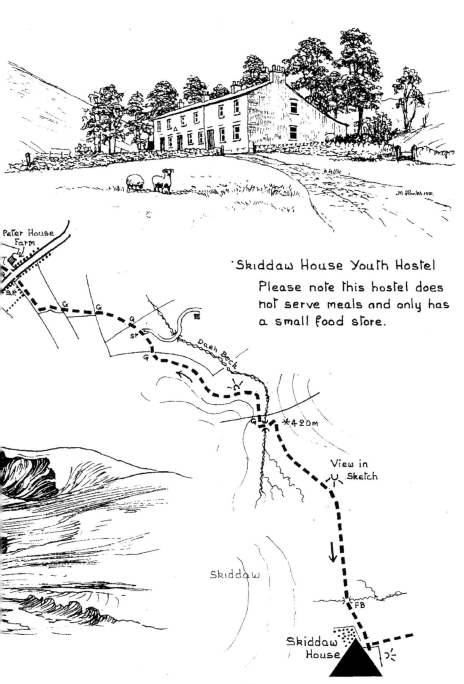

Skiddaw House Youth Hostel

Please note this hostel does not serve meals and only has a small food store.

Walking route between
Keswick YH and Carrock Fell YH
e page 91

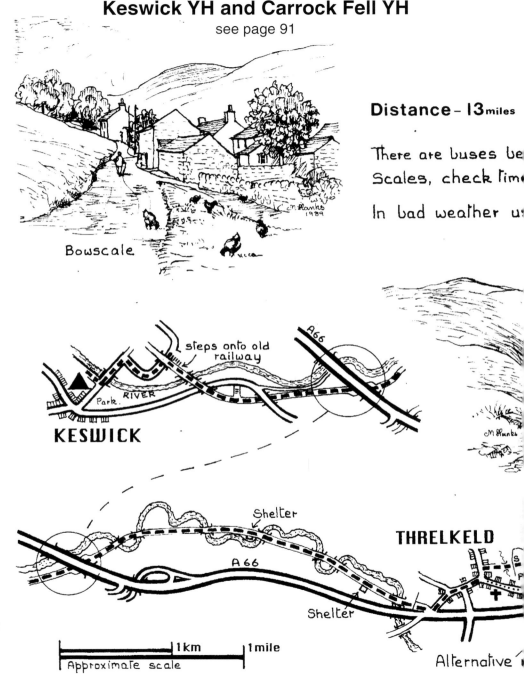

Bowscale

Distance – 13 miles

There are buses be...
Scales, check tim...

In bad weather u...

steps onto old railway

A66

KESWICK
Park. RIVER

Shelter

THRELKELD

A66

Shelter

1km   1mile
Approximate scale

Alternative

96

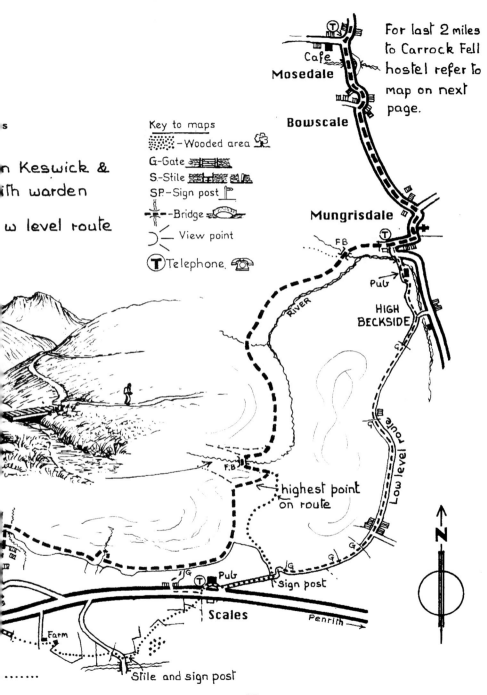

For last 2 miles to Carrock Fell hostel refer to map on next page.

Cafe
Mosedale

Bowscale

Key to maps
- Wooded area
- G - Gate
- S - Stile
- SP - Sign post
- Bridge
- View point
- T Telephone.

Mungrisdale

s

n Keswick &
ith warden

w level route

FB

Pub

HIGH
BECKSIDE

RIVER

Low level route

F.B.

highest point
on route

N

F.B.

Pub

Sign post

G

G

Scales

Penrith →

Farm

Stile and sign post

97

Walking route between
Keswick YH and Carrock Fell YH
via Skiddaw House YH

see page 91

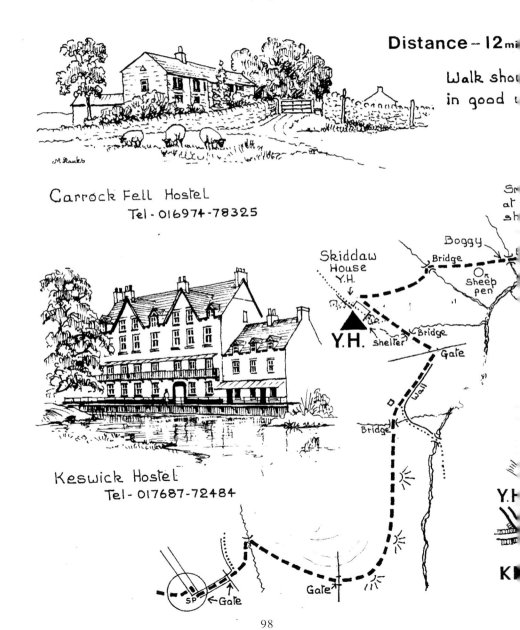

Distance – 12 mi

Walk shou
in good u

Carrock Fell Hostel
Tel · 016974 · 78325

Keswick Hostel
Tel · 017687 · 72484

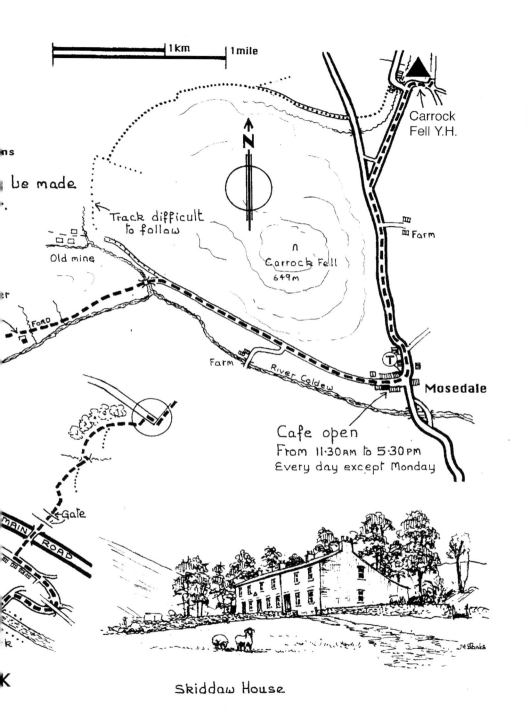

1 km   1 mile

ns

be made

Track difficult
to follow

Old mine

r

Ford

N

Carrock Fell
649m

Farm

Carrock
Fell Y.H.

Farm

River Coldew

T

Mosedale

Cafe open
From 11·30 AM to 5·30 PM
Every day except Monday

Gate

MAIN ROAD

k

K

Skiddaw House

99

Walking route between Carrock Fell YH and Skiddaw House YH

see page 91

Approximate distance by both routes 7.5 miles, 12 Km.

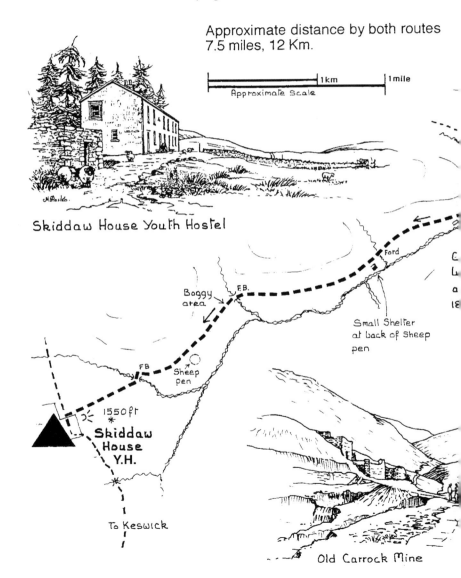

1km   1mile

Approximate Scale

Skiddaw House Youth Hostel

Ford

Boggy area   F.B.

Small Shelter at back of Sheep pen

FB
Sheep pen

1550ft

Skiddaw House Y.H.

To Keswick

Old Carrock Mine

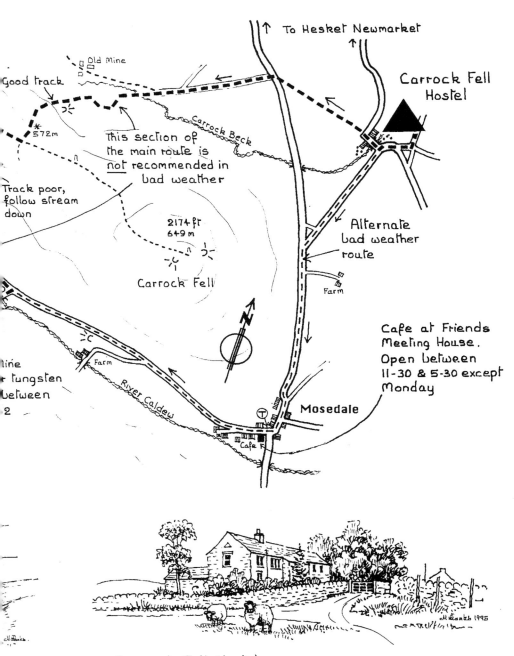

To Hesket Newmarket

Old Mine

Good track

Carrock Fell Hostel

572m

Carrock Beck

This section of the main route is not recommended in bad weather

Track poor, follow stream down

2174 ft 649 m

Carrock Fell

Alternate bad weather route

Farm

Cafe at Friends Meeting House. Open between 11-30 & 5-30 except Monday

line tungsten between 2

Farm

River Caldew

Mosedale

Cafe

Carrock Fell Hostel Tel- 016974-78325

Walks around Carrock Fell YH

(The maps are on pages 104/107)

Some of the walks between Skiddaw YH and Carrock Fell YH can also be incorporated in a variety of circular routes around Carrock Fell, West Fell and High Pike which Martyn highlights on his map. Some of these are useful alternatives when poor weather precludes walking to the higher fells.

To the north lie the villages of Caldbeck and Hesket Newmarket, which offer a lower alternative to the fells. John Peel, the huntsman, is buried at Caldbeck. Both villages are attractive and the house with a tall chimney seen in Martyn's drawing of Caldbeck used to be a brewery. The Old Crown Inn in Hesket Newmarket continues this tradition. This walk is about 8 miles (12.8km) in length.

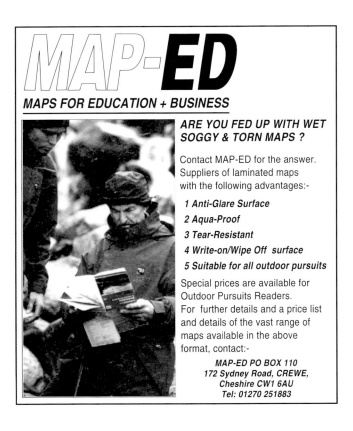

Keswick YH to Derwentwater YH, Borrowdale YH and Honister Hause YH
(The map is on pages 108/109)

Derwentwater YH is only a couple of miles from Keswick and there is a choice of a lakeside walk or by launch. In fact the launch goes further down Derwent Water if you prefer a longer cruise on the lake.

To reach Borrowdale YH there is a choice of routes. You can walk from Derwentwater YH to Watendlath, using both the minor road and then a footpath to reach the hamlet. From here it is a short distance to Rosthwaite and the youth hostel. Alternatively, there is a lakeside path on the west side of Derwent Water which leads to Grange village. From here a path keeps close to the River Derwent and brings you to Borrowdale YH.

This path continues around to Seatoller and climbs up to Honister Hause YH on the top of Honister Pass. There is a more direct route to Seatoller from Grange via Broadslack Gill. Rising into the foothills of Dale Head Fell, this route is more scenic.

Thirlmere YH to Derwentwater YH and Keswick YH
(The map is on pages 110/111)

Thirlmere, which is a reservoir and provides water for Manchester, is surrounded by forest. The first 2 miles (3.2km) are along a lane down the west side of the lake, but the views are often impeded by trees. At Cockrigg Crags there is a gap in the forest where a path climbs over High Tove to Watendlath. It is boggy in places, requiring suitable footwear.

From Watendlath both a path and minor road run down towards Derwent Water. The path joins the lane near Ashness Wood where there is a view point overlooking the lake. Ashness Bridge is a very popular view point too and appears on numerous postcards. Derwentwater YH is at the bottom of the road. From here there is a lakeside path to Keswick or you can catch the launch down to Keswick on the lake.

Thirlmere YH to Skiddaw House YH
(The map is on pages 112/113)

The flat valley of St John's in the Vale has a path linking Thirlmere with Threlkeld. It is an easy stroll through the fields. From Threlkeld the lane to the Blencathra Centre is taken. Here the road peters out and a path up the Glenderaterra Beck leads onto the fells to join the Cumbria Way path. This passes Skiddaw House at a height of 1,550ft (470m), nearly 1,100ft (330m) above Threlkeld.

Walks around
Carrock Fell YH: Map 1
see page 102

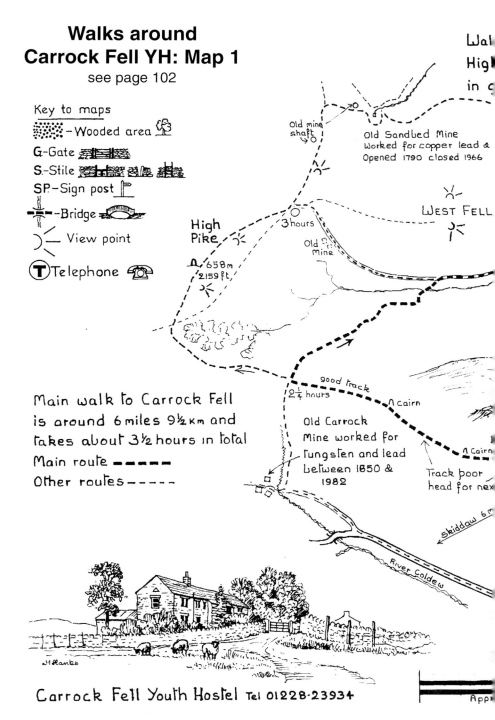

Key to maps

▓▓ — Wooded area 🌳

G — Gate 🚪

S — Stile 🚧

SP — Sign post 🚩

✝ — Bridge 🌉

)‿ View point

(T) Telephone ☎

Old mine shaft

Old Sandbed Mine
Worked for copper lead &
Opened 1790 closed 1966

WEST FELL

High
Pike

3 hours

Old
Mine

△ 658m
2159 ft

Main walk to Carrock Fell
is around 6 miles 9½km and
takes about 3½ hours in total

Main route ━ ━ ━ ━

Other routes ─ ─ ─ ─

good track
2¼ hours

⌃ cairn

Old Carrock
Mine worked for
Tungsten and lead
between 1850 &
1982

⌃ Cairn

Track poor
head for nex

Skiddaw 6 m

River Coldew

Carrock Fell Youth Hostel Tel 01228-23934

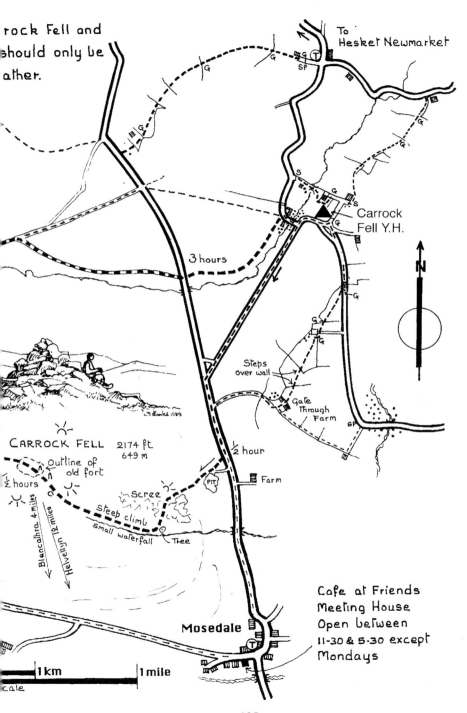

rock Fell and
should only be
ather.

To
Hesket Newmarket

Carrock
Fell Y.H.

N

3 hours

Steps
over wall

Gate
Through
Farm

CARROCK FELL   2174 ft
                649 m

Outline of
old fort

½ hours

½ hour

Blencathra 4 miles
Helvellyn 12 miles

Scree

Steep climb

Small waterfall

Tree

PIT

Farm

Cafe at Friends
Meeting House
Open between
11·30 & 5·30 except
Mondays

Mosedale

1km   1mile

cale

Walks around
Carrock Fell YH: Map 2
see page 102

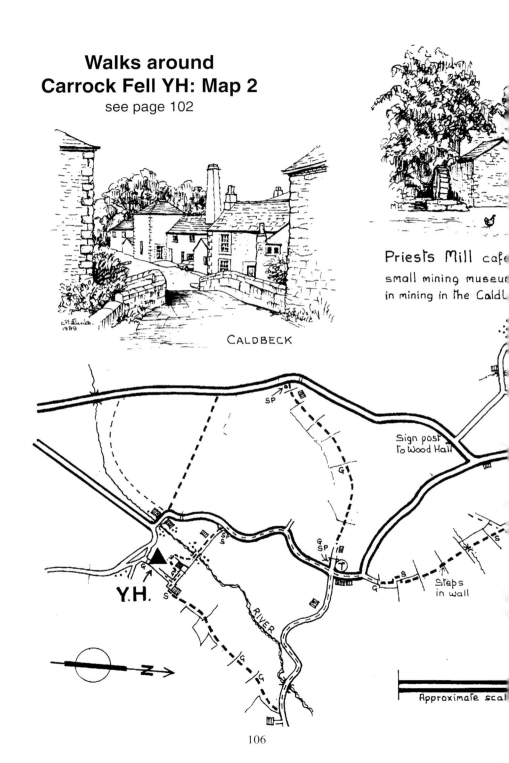

CALDBECK

Priests Mill cafe
small mining museum
in mining in the Caldb

Sign post
To Wood Hall

SP

G

G
SP

T

Steps
in wall

Y.H.

RIVER

G

G

N

Approximate scal

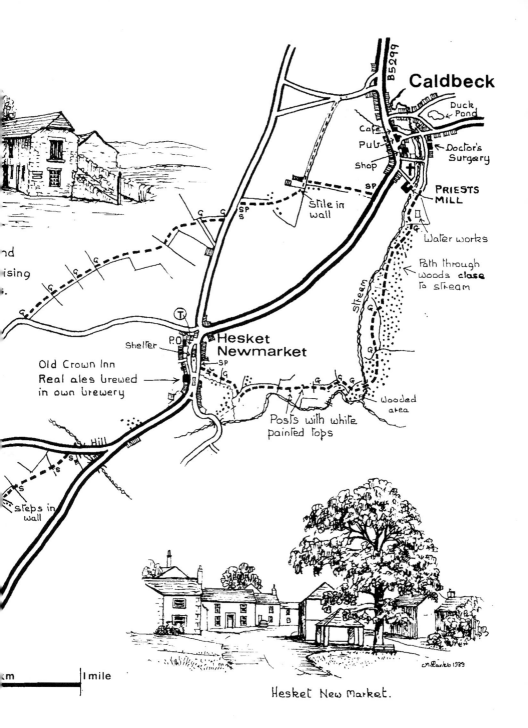

Caldbeck

Duck Pond

Café

Pub

Shop

Doctor's Surgery

PRIESTS MILL

Water works

Path through woods **close** to stream

Stile in wall

Stream

Hesket Newmarket

Shelter

P.O.

SP

Old Crown Inn
Real ales brewed
in own brewery

Posts with white painted tops

Wooded area

Hill

Steps in wall

km ⊢ 1 mile

Hesket New Market.

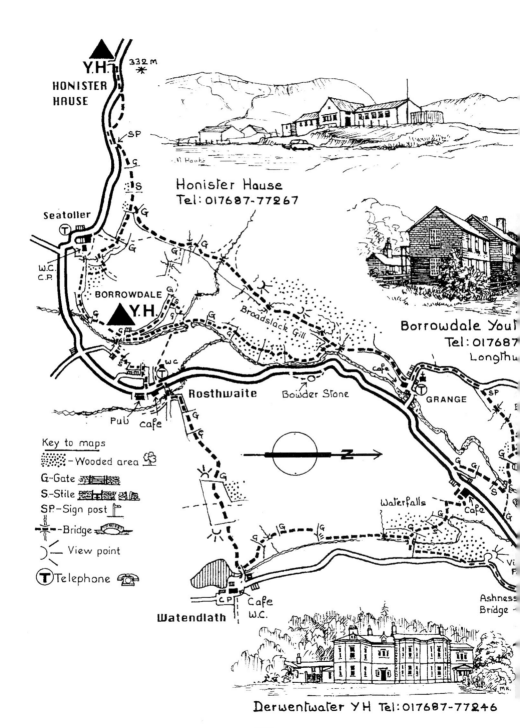

Y.H.
HONISTER
HAUSE

332 m

SP

G

S

Honister House
Tel: 017687-77267

Seatoller

W.C.
C.P.

BORROWDALE **Y.H.**

Broadslack Gill

Borrowdale Youl
Tel: 017687
Longthw

Cafe

GRANGE

SP

Rosthwaite

Bowder Stone

Pub Cafe

G

Key to maps
—Wooded area
G-Gate
S-Stile
SP-Sign post
—Bridge
View point
Telephone

N

Waterfalls

Cafe

G

Vi

Ashness
Bridge

CP Cafe
W.C.

Watendlath

Derwentwater YH Tel: 017687-77246

108

Walking routes between Keswick YH, Derwentwater YH, BorrowdaleYH and Honister YH

see page 103

Approximate distances by footpaths to hostels

	Direct	via Portinscale	via Watendlath
Longthwaite	7½ miles 12 km	8 miles 13 km	7¾ miles 12 km
Honister	8 miles 13 km	8 miles 14 km	10 miles 16 km
Derwentwater	2½ miles 4 km	6 miles 10 km	

Broadslack Gill
looking towards Skiddaw

Launches sail about each hour
From Easter to Oct 15
10am to 5.30P
10am to 8pm in Summer

DERWENTWATER

Car Park

SP

PORTINSCALE

Food Store

Derwent Bank

SP

Launch

Cafe
Park

Y.H.

KESWICK
Y.H.
Tel: 017687-724066

1km   1mile
Approximate scale

Walking route between Thirlmere YH, Derwentwater YH and Keswick YH

see page 103

The section of this route between Thirlmere and Watendlath should only be made in good weather, unless well equipped

Thirlmere to Keswick about 9 mile. 14½ km

Ashness

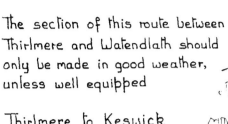

Derwentwater Youth Hostel
Tel · 017687 - 77246

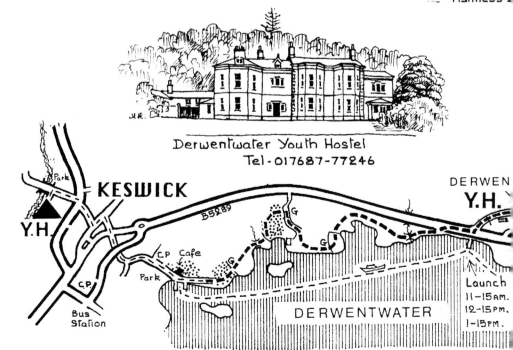

KESWICK

Y.H.

Park

Bus Station

C.P.

Park

C.P. Cafe

B5289

DERWEN
Y.H.

Launch
11 – 15am.
12 – 15pm.
1 – 15pm.

DERWENTWATER

110

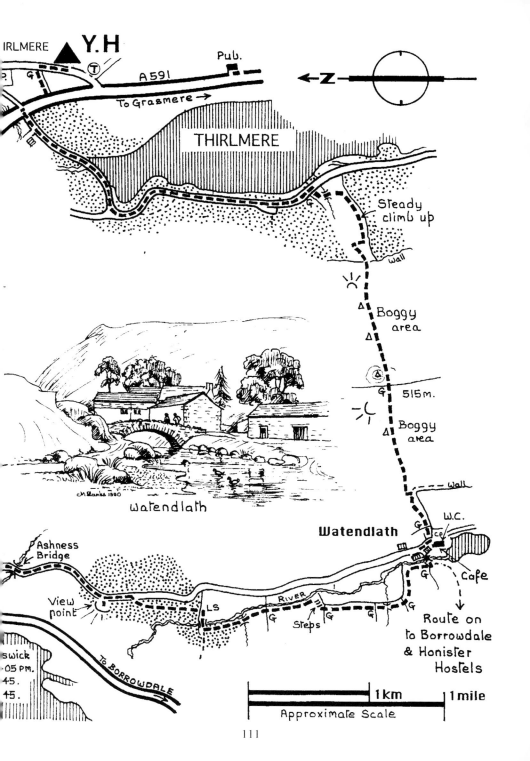

IRLMERE ▲ Y.H

Pub.

A591

To Grasmere →

←Z

THIRLMERE

Steady climb up

Wall

Boggy area

515m.

Boggy area

Wall

Watendlath

W.C.

Watendlath

Cafe

Ashness Bridge

View point

LS

RIVER

Steps

Route on to Borrowdale & Honister Hostels

swick
·05 pm.
45.
45.

To BORROWDALE

1km   1 mile

Approximate Scale

C.M. Banks 1990

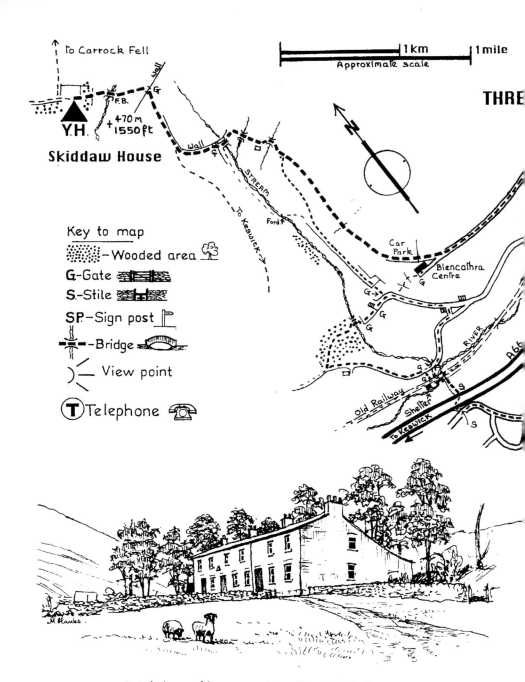

Skiddaw House Youth Hostel

All usual simple hostel facilities and small store.

Walking route between
Thirlmere YH and Skiddaw House YH
see page 103

Distance via Threlkeld 9miles 14kms --
Direct route 8½ miles 13kms ------

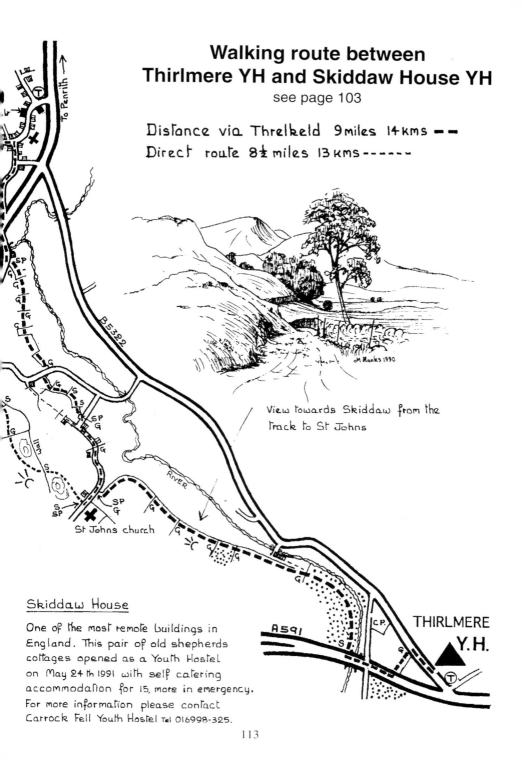

View towards Skiddaw from the track to St Johns

St Johns church

River

B5322

To Penrith →

A591

C.P.

THIRLMERE
Y.H.

Skiddaw House

One of the most remote buildings in
England. This pair of old shepherds
cottages opened as a Youth Hostel
on May 24th 1991 with self catering
accommodation for 15, more in emergency.
For more information please contact
Carrock Fell Youth Hostel Tel 016998-325.

113

Thirlmere YH to Carrock Fell YH

(The maps are on pages 116/119)

The same route into Threlkeld is taken as for the route to Skiddaw House YH. Here the path joins the low level Keswick YH to Carrock Fell YH route.

Thirlmere YH to Keswick YH (low level route)

(The map is on pages 120/121)

A choice of routes is suggested by Martyn and some can be used as circular walks from either Thirlmere or Keswick YHs. The path to Threlkeld allows you then to walk to Keswick on the former railway line. Alternatively you can leave this path near Tewet Tarn to follow a minor lane to Castlerigg Stone Circle. From here you can take a path via Castlerigg to enter Keswick along Springs Road, or walk down the road directly into town.

A further route heads more directly to the stone circle. It crosses fields first on one side of the A591 and then on the other.

Thirlmere YH to Borrowdale YH and Honister Hause YH

(The map is on pages 122/123)

This route takes the path to Watendlath (described above on the **Thirlmere YH to Derwentwater YH and Keswick YH** route). From here it goes on to Rosthwaite on the path described under **Keswick to Derwentwater, Borrowdale and Honister Hause YHs**.

Walks around Borrowdale YH

(The maps are on pages 124/127)

Martyn suggests both a high and low level route on his first map. For the energetic there is the path which runs up the valley to the top of Honister Pass. Here a path goes due north up to the top of Dale Head via the disused slate quarries. It's a good climb to the top (2,485ft, 753m above sea level). From here it's downhill via Tongue Gill back to Longthwaite. This route should only be attempted in good weather and if you are well equipped.

For a less testing walk, take the road from Seatoller to Seathwaite. At Seathwaite Bridge take the path to the right of the river and follow it up into Sty Head Gill to a ford above Taylorgill Force (a waterfall). Ford the stream and descend down to Stockley Bridge. Cross Grains Gill, walk down to Seathwaite and on to Longthwaite. Except for Sty Head Gill, this walk is fairly flat.

A variety of walks are suggested by Martyn on his second map, although some are dependent on good weather. The main route goes to Grange and then up the Watendlath Beck to Watendlath. It returns via Bowdergate Gill and Rosthwaite. A more direct route from Grange via Jopplety How and Dock Tarn is shown as a good weather route to Stonethwaite.

A further short and low level route is through Stonethwaite to Langstrath Beck, returning down the far side of the valley to Rosthwaite. Between the hostel and Grange is Castle Crag. The river path can be followed downstream to here with a return up Broadslack Gill and a descent to Johnny Wood at the rear of the hostel.

Walking route between
Thirlmere YH and Carrock Fell YH: Map 1

see page 114

Approximate distance 13 miles, 21 Km

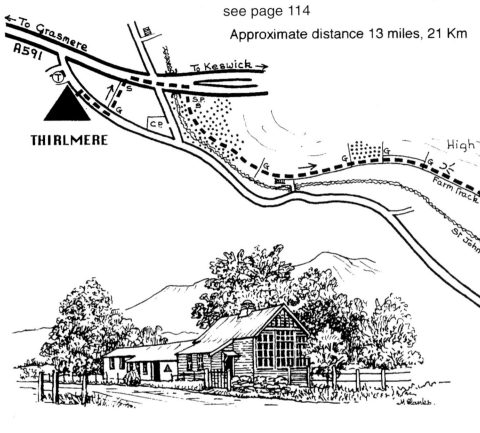

To Grasmere

A591

THIRLMERE

To Keswick →

S.P.
S

C.P.

High

Farm Track

St Johns

Key to maps

▒▒ –Wooded area

G–Gate

S.–Stile

S.P.–Sign post

–Bridge

View point

T Telephone

Thirlmere Youth Hostel

Tel – 017687 – 73224

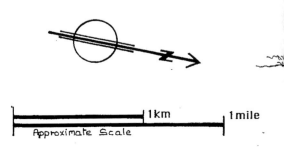

1km

1mile

Approximate Scale

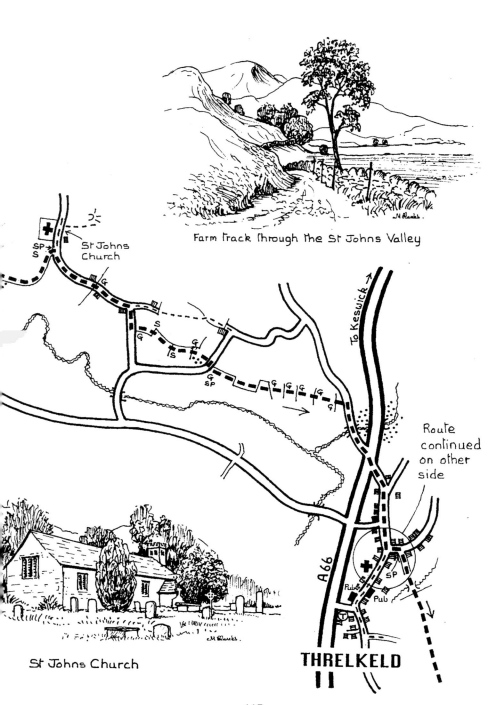

Farm Track Through the St Johns Valley

St Johns Church
SP S

St Johns Church

To Keswick

Route continued on other side

A66

THRELKELD

Pub

Pub

SP

117

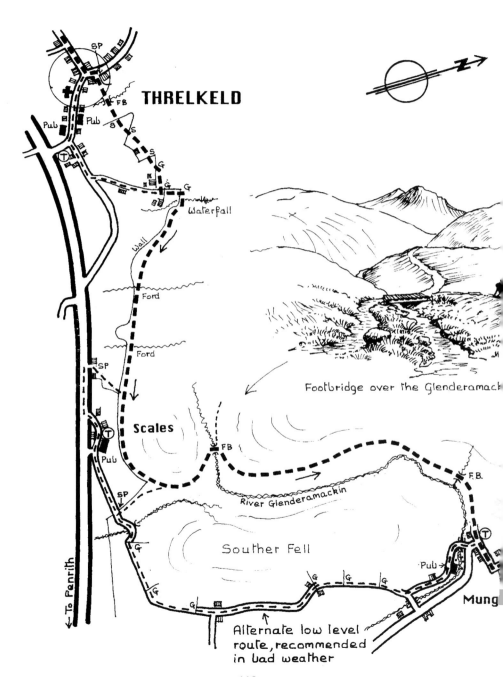

THRELKELD

Pub   Pub

FB

Waterfall

Wall

Ford

Ford

SP

Scales

Footbridge over the Glenderamack

FB

River Glenderamackin

F.B.

Souther Fell

Pub

SP

To Penrith

Mung

Alternate low level
route, recommended
in bad weather

Walking route between
Thirlmere YH and Carrock Fell YH: Map 2
see page 114

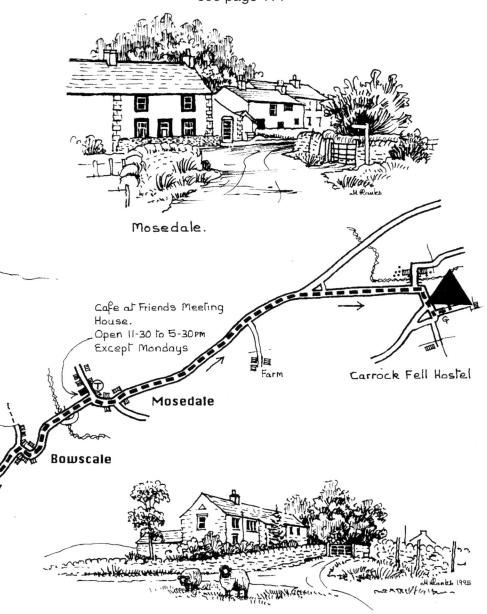

Mosedale.

Cafe at Friends Meeting House.
Open 11-30 to 5-30PM
Except Mondays

Farm

Carrock Fell Hostel

Mosedale

Bowscale

Carrock Fell Hostel Tel- 016974-78325

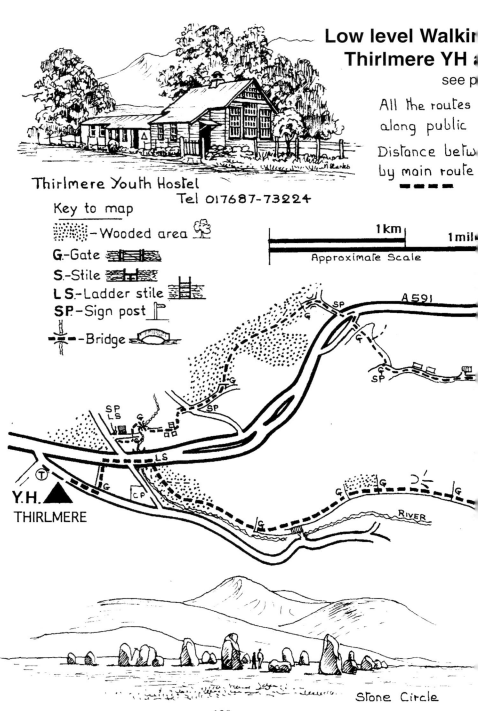

Low level Walkir
Thirlmere YH
see p

All the routes
along public

Distance betw
by main route

Thirlmere Youth Hostel

Tel 017687-73224

Key to map

- ░░░ – Wooded area 🌳
- **G**.–Gate
- **S**.–Stile
- **L.S**.–Ladder stile
- **S.P**.–Sign post ⌐
- ╪ –Bridge

1km
1mil
Approximate Scale

A591

SP

SP

SP
LS

SP

LS

G

T

Y.H.
THIRLMERE

CP

G

G

G

G

G

RIVER

Stone Circle

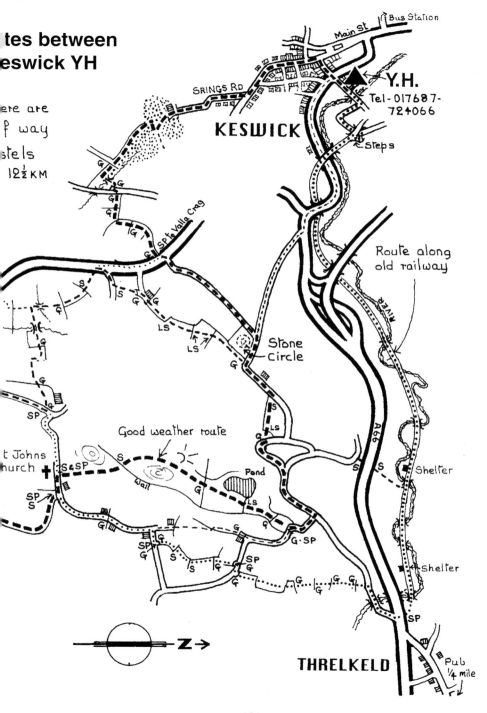

tes between
eswick YH

ere are
f way
tels
12½ KM

Bus Station

Main St

SRINGS RD

KESWICK

Y.H.
Tel- 017687-
724066

Steps

SP to Valla Crag

Route along
old railway

RIVER

Stone
Circle

Good weather route

t Johns
hurch

Wall

Pond

Shelter

A66

Shelter

SP

Z →

THRELKELD

Pub
¼ mile

Walking route between Thirlmere YH, Borrowdale YH and Honister Hause YH

see page 115

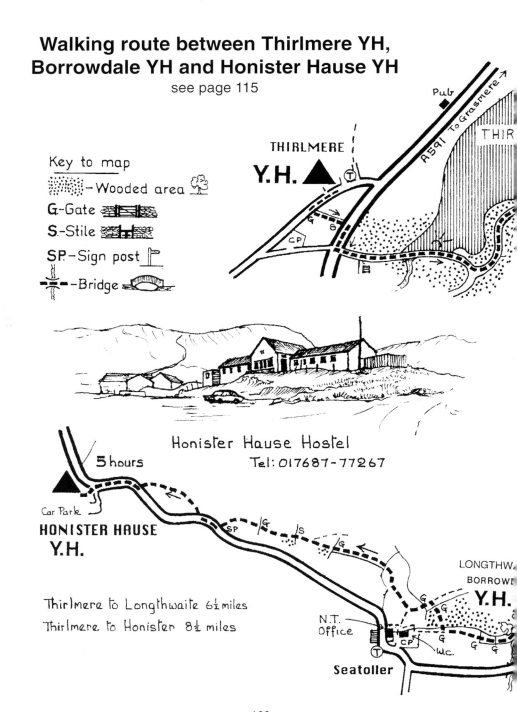

Key to map

- ░░░ – Wooded area
- G–Gate
- S.–Stile
- SP.–Sign post
- ╪═╪ –Bridge

THIRLMERE Y.H.

Pub
A591 To Grasmere
THIR

Honister Hause Hostel
Tel: 017687-77267

5 hours

Car Park
HONISTER HAUSE Y.H.

Thirlmere to Longthwaite 6¼ miles
Thirlmere to Honister 8¼ miles

N.T. Office

Seatoller

LONGTHW.
BORROWI
Y.H.

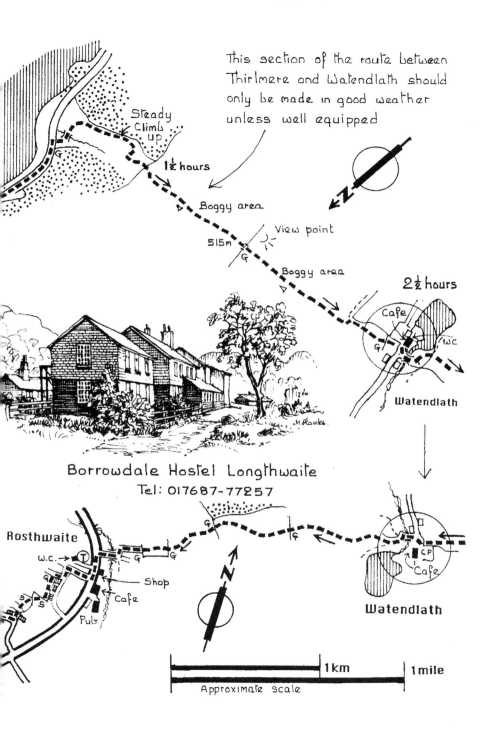

This section of the route between Thirlmere and Watendlath should only be made in good weather unless well equipped

Steady Climb up

1½ hours

Boggy area

515m View point

Boggy area

2½ hours

Cafe

WC

Watendlath

Borrowdale Hostel Longthwaite
Tel: 017687-77257

Rosthwaite

W.C.

Shop

Cafe

Pub

Watendlath

CP

Cafe

1km   1mile
Approximate scale

123

Total distance of this walk 6 miles 9 km ▬ ▬ ▬

To Keswick
← B5289

To Tarn at Leaves ⅝ mile 1km ↘
Track poor in places

Borrowdale Y.H.

Old saw mill

Farm

CP WC

T

SEATOLLER

Steep climb through old slate tips

505m

Tarn

Boggy area

Old fence posts

←This walk should only be made if well equipped and in good weather ↓

Dale Head 753m

YH HONISTER

1km   1mile
Approximate scale

Seathwaite

124

Walks from Borrowdale YH

see page 115

Key to map

⋯⋯ — Wooded area 🌳

G—Gate

S.—Stile

SP.—Sign post

— Bridge

)—(View point

(T) Telephone ☎

Borrowdale Hostel Longthwaite
Tel: 017687-77257

SEATHWAITE
W.C. (T)
café Grains Gill

Stockley Bridge

Easy climb

Taylorgill Force Waterfalls

Scramble over rocks.

Ford

Sly Head Gill

Total distance of this walk 6½ miles 10½ km

Old Saw mill

Stockley Bridge

cN Franks 1991

125

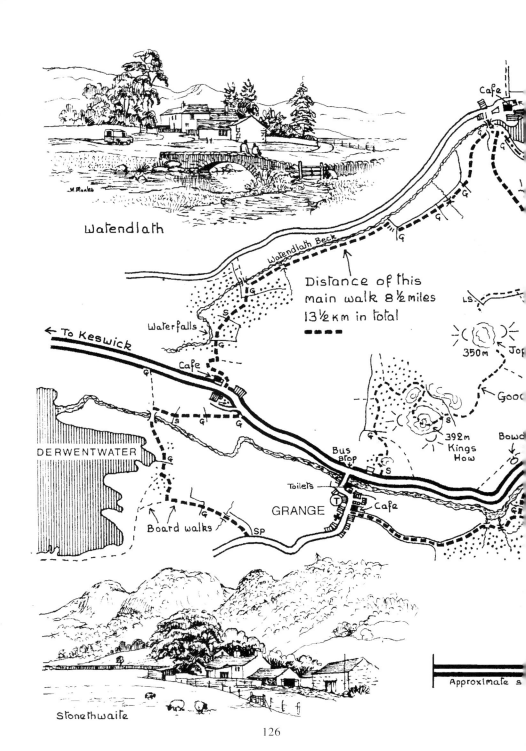

Watendlath

Cafe

Watendlath Beck

Distance of this
main walk 8½ miles
13½ km in total

350m

392m
Kings
How

Waterfalls

← To Keswick

Cafe

DERWENTWATER

Board walks

SP

Bus
stop

Toilets

GRANGE

Cafe

Stonethwaite

Approximate s

126

Walks from Borrowdale YH

see page 115

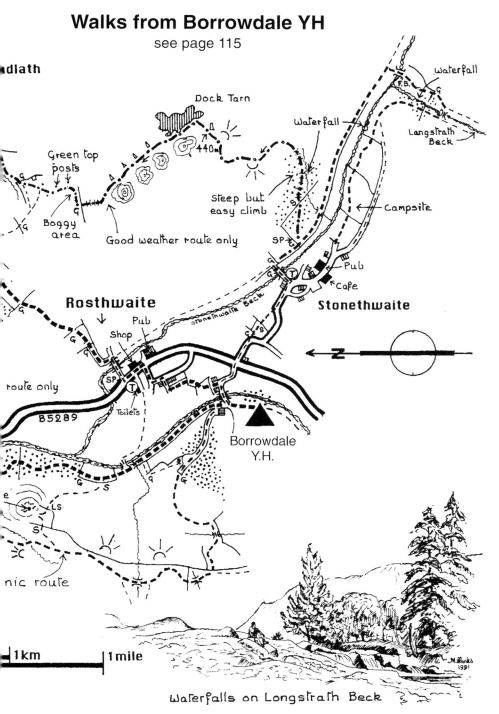

Waterfalls on Longsfrath Beck

Walks from Buttermere YH

Buttermere
(The map is on pages 130/131)

Buttermere Lake has a beautiful setting between the fells and is only 5 miles (8 km) to walk around. The path is close to the water's edge on each side. At the village end, it crosses through the fields on a track which runs down from the village to the far western end of the lake. At the diagonally opposite end, the path diverts around by Gatesgarth Farm where there is a carpark.

Crummock Water
(The maps are on pages 132/135)

If you have reached Buttermere YH having walked down the side of Buttermere, you may prefer an alternative lake for a circular tour. Buttermere village has another lake to offer—Crummock Water. There is a lake-side walk if you want to keep to a low level route.

Alternatively, a path climbs up the far (western) side of Mellbreak Fell before dropping down into Loweswater. Refreshments are available at lunchtime at the Kirkstile Inn. Proceeding down the road from the pub to the river, take the path to the right through Lanthwaite Wood to rejoin the lake. Upon reaching the B5289, you can return by road or, better still, walk up Rannerdale before dropping back down into Buttermere village.

A shorter route follows the Mill Beck from Buttermere down to Crummock Water and then bears right along the lake to the B5289. To avoid the road, a path climbs up the hillside a little before dropping back to the road and skirting the outcrop of Rannerdale Knotts. The path climbs up the gentle gradient of Rannerdale before descending into the village. This is a fairly easy route taking about three hours, and has many fine views on the way.

Wast Water YH to Black Sail Hut YH and Buttermere YH

(The maps are on pages 136/139)

Take the quiet lane which runs up the side of Wast Water from the hostel. The views are superb, both up the lake to Yewbarrow on the left, Great Gable in the middle and Lingmell on the right, and across the lake to Ingill Head.

Upon reaching Wasdale Head with its hotel, pub, cafe and shop the path heads into Mosedale, crossing the beck near to the shop. Keeping the river to your left, the path is relatively flat before it bears up to the right and over the Black Sail Pass. To the left is Pillar and to the right, Kirk Fell. Once over the top, it is a quick descent to Black Sail Hut.

If you are proceeding on to Buttermere, it's a leisurely walk from Black Sail. The path goes down the valley to Ennerdale Forest and then turns up and over Scarth Gap, an easy uphill walk. At the top of the gap, the dramatic view of Upper Ennerdale is replaced by another down to Buttermere. The path drops down to the lake and follows the south side to reach Buttermere village.

Grasmere YH to Patterdale YH

(The maps are on pages 140/143)

If you are staying at Butterlip How YH, take the lane to nearby Thorney How YH and continue up the road to reach the A591. Cross this and take the path to Hause Gap between Seat Sandal and Fairfield Fells. Behind rises Dollywagon Pike, above which looms Helvellyn. Take the footbridge near a water tank; the path then climbs up with the Tongue Gill stream to your left. To the right, the valley side rises up to Great Rigg, with Fairfield to the north. The path climbs steadily up the valley on a good track to reach Hause Gap, where it descends past Grisedale Tarn into Grisedale.

Just beyond the climbing hut (Ruthwaite Lodge), the path branches, one running down each side of the river. They are linked by a short path at the bottom of the dale, so you can take your choice. Upon reaching the Patterdale end of the valley, you can walk down to the main road and turn right for the youth hostel. Alternatively, a path climbs up the valley side for a short distance before levelling out and then dropping down to the A592 close to the hostel. This path has the advantage of better views of Ullswater.

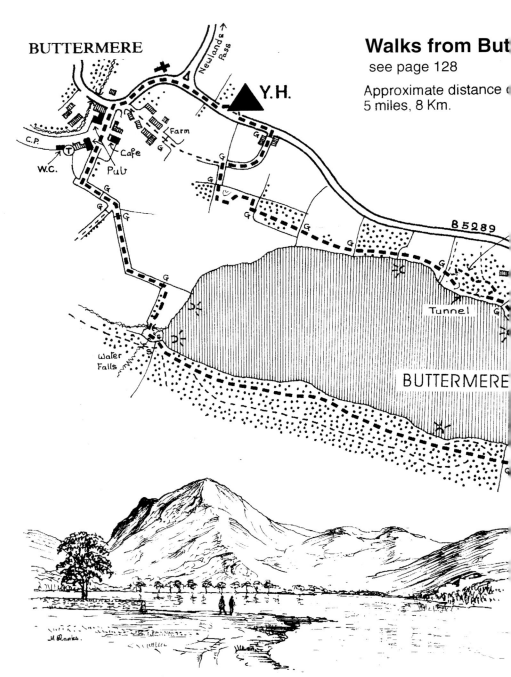

BUTTERMERE

Walks from But[termere]

see page 128

Approximate distance [is]
5 miles, 8 Km.

Newlands Pass →

Y.H.

Farm

C.P.

W.C.

T

Cafe

Pub

G

B 5289

Tunnel

Water Falls

BUTTERMERE

M. Banks.

View of Fleetwith Pike from the lake path

ircular route

rary
rsion

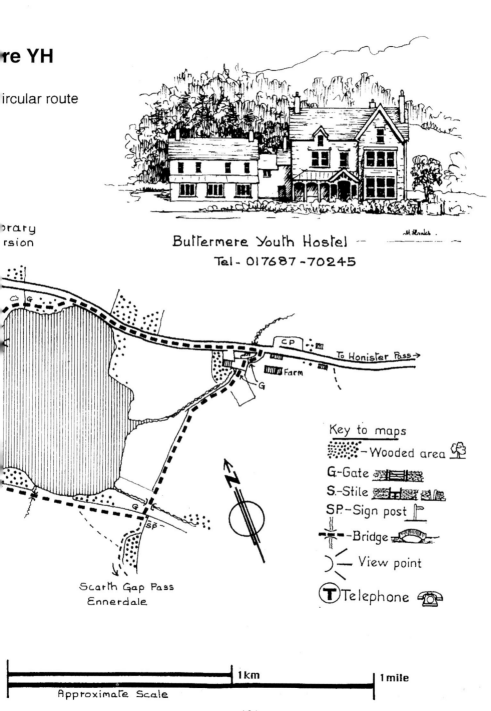

Buttermere Youth Hostel
Tel - 017687 - 70245

Scarth Gap Pass
Ennerdale

To Honister Pass →

CP

Farm

Key to maps

⋯ - Wooded area 🌳

G - Gate

S. - Stile

SP - Sign post

━╪━ - Bridge

)⟨ — View point

ⓣ Telephone 📞

1km   1mile

Approximate Scale

Walks from Buttermere YH

see page 128

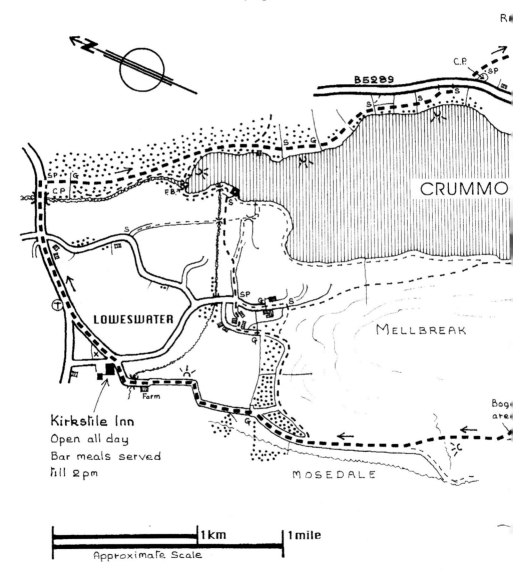

R

C.P.
SP

B5289

CRUMMO

SP · G
C P

E.B.

S

SP

MELLBREAK

LOWESWATER

T

Farm

Bog
are

Kirkstile Inn
Open all day
Bar meals served
till 2pm

MOSEDALE

| 1km | 1mile |

Approximate Scale

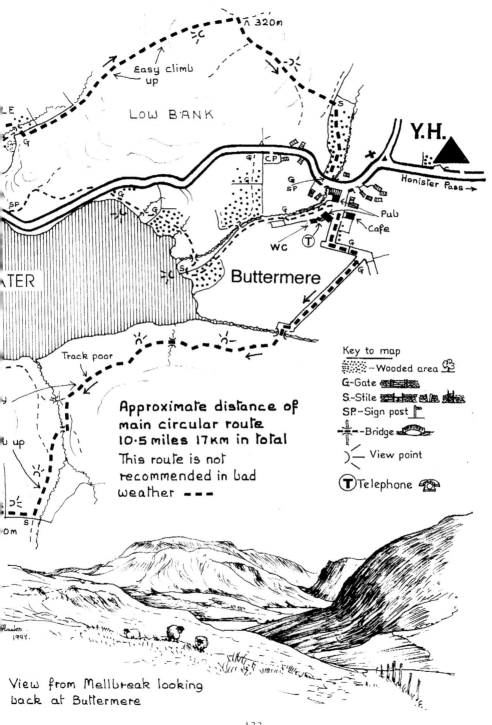

320m

Easy climb up

LOW BANK

Y.H.

Honister Pass →

G

CP

SP

G

SP

G

Pub

Cafe

WC (T)

Buttermere

G

SP

G

Track poor

up

Approximate distance of main circular route 10·5 miles 17km in total
This route is not recommended in bad weather ‑ ‑ ‑

Key to map
░░ –Wooded area 🌳
G.–Gate ▦
S.–Stile ▦
SP.–Sign post ⌐
✝–Bridge 🌉
)‑ – View point
(T)Telephone ☎

View from Mellbreak looking back at Buttermere

133

Walks from Buttermere YH

see page 128

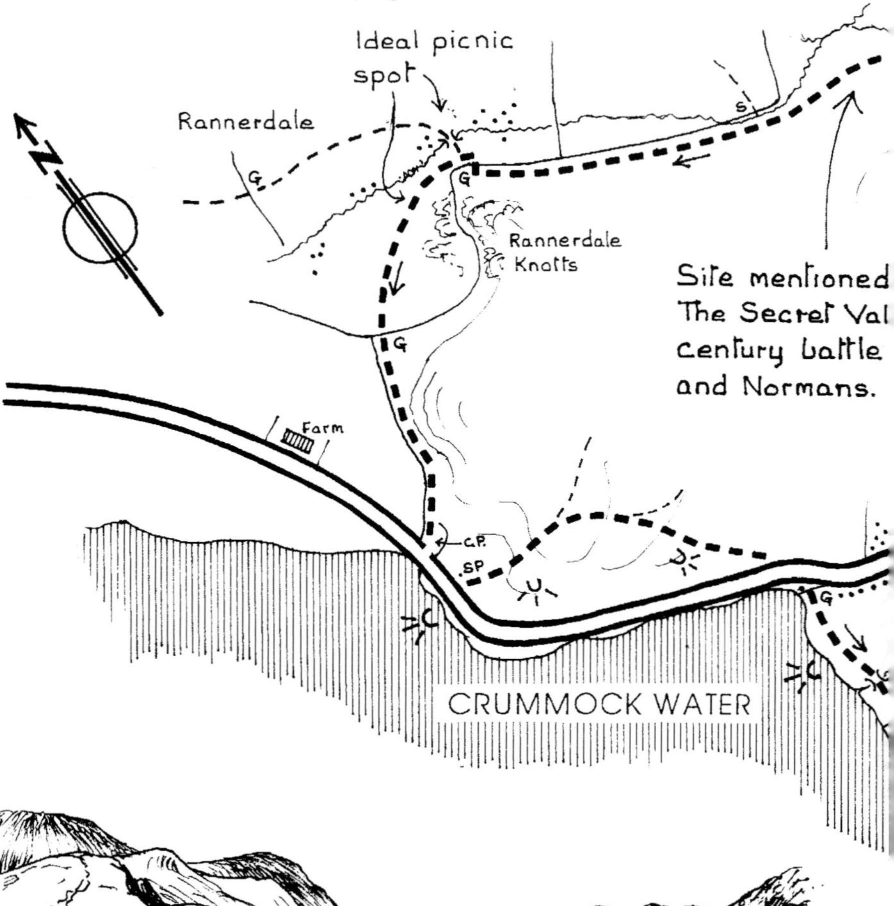

Ideal picnic spot

Rannerdale

S

G

G

Rannerdale Knotts

Site mentioned
The Secret Val
century battle
and Normans.

N

Farm

C.P.

SP

U

C

G

C

CRUMMOCK WATER

View looking down Rannerdale

N.Banks
1997

Approximate Sc

134

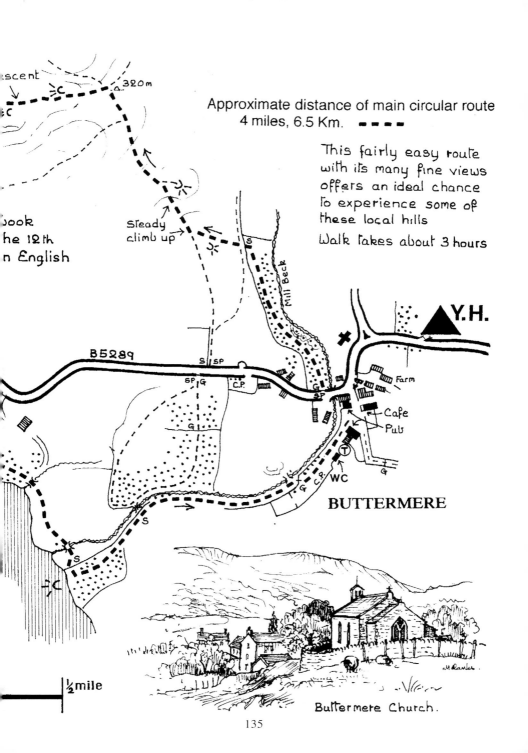

scent

C
320m

Approximate distance of main circular route
4 miles, 6.5 Km. ▬ ▬ ▬ ▬

This fairly easy route
with its many fine views
offers an ideal chance
to experience some of
these local hills

Walk takes about 3 hours

Steady
climb up

ook
he 12th
n English

Mill Beck

▲ Y.H.

B5289

S SP

SP G

C.P.

G

Farm

G

Cafe
Pub

T

G C.P.

WC

BUTTERMERE

S

S

½ mile

Buttermere Church.

135

Walking route between Wast Water YH, Black Sail YH and Buttermere YH: Map 1

see page 129

Approximate distances
Black Sail Hostel 6.5 miles, 10 Km.
Buttermere Hostel 10.5 miles, 17 Km.

This route is not recommended in bad weather unless well equipped

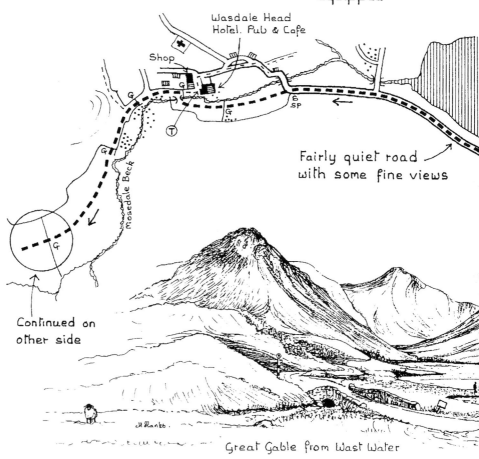

Wasdale Head
Hotel. Pub & Cafe

Shop

Mosedale Beck

Fairly quiet road with some fine views

Continued on other side

M Planks.

Great Gable from Wast Water

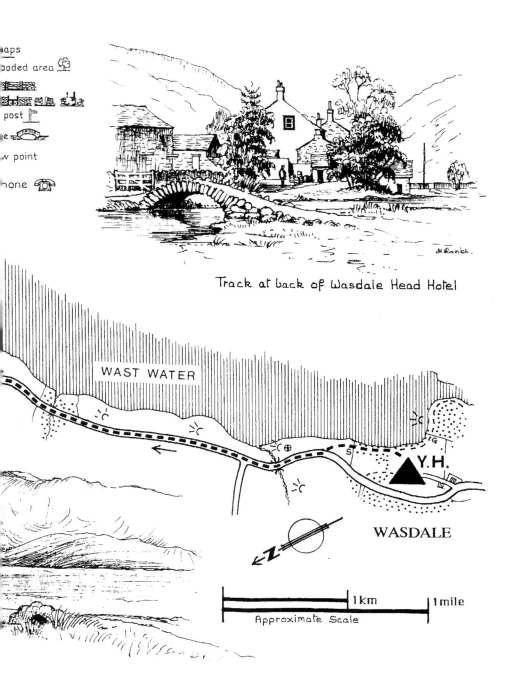

maps

ooded area 🌲

post 🏁

e

w point

hone ☎

Track at back of Wasdale Head Hotel

WAST WATER

Y.H.

WASDALE

N

1km 1mile
Approximate Scale

137

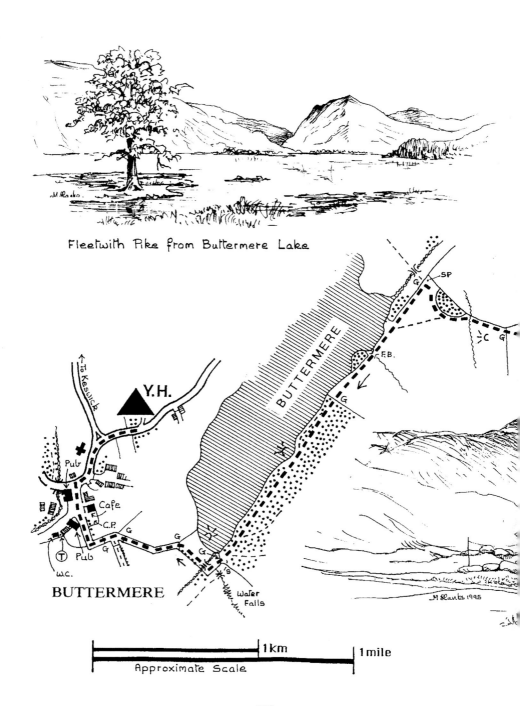

Fleetwith Pike from Buttermere Lake

BUTTERMERE

Y.H.

To Keswick

Pub

Cafe

C.P.

Pub

W.C.

Water Falls

SP

F.B.

1km   1mile

Approximate Scale

M Planks 1995

Walking route between
Wast Water YH, Black Sail YH
and Buttermere YH: Map 2
see page 129

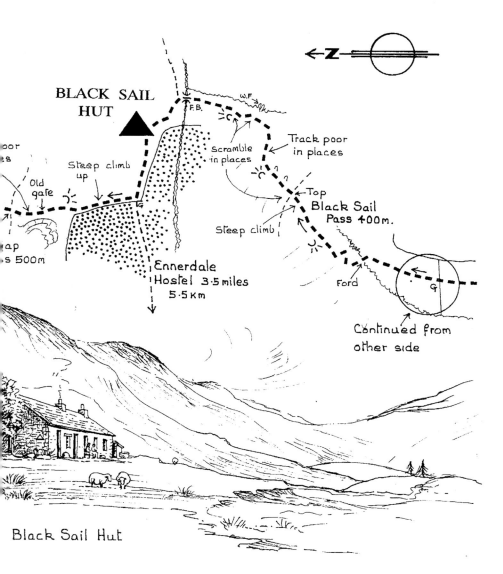

←Z ⊖

BLACK SAIL HUT

W.F.

F.B.

Track poor in places

Scramble in places

oor
s

Steep climb up

Old gate

Top
Black Sail
Pass 400m.

Steep climb

ap
s 500m

Ennerdale
Hostel 3·5 miles
5·5 km

Ford
G

Continued from other side

Black Sail Hut

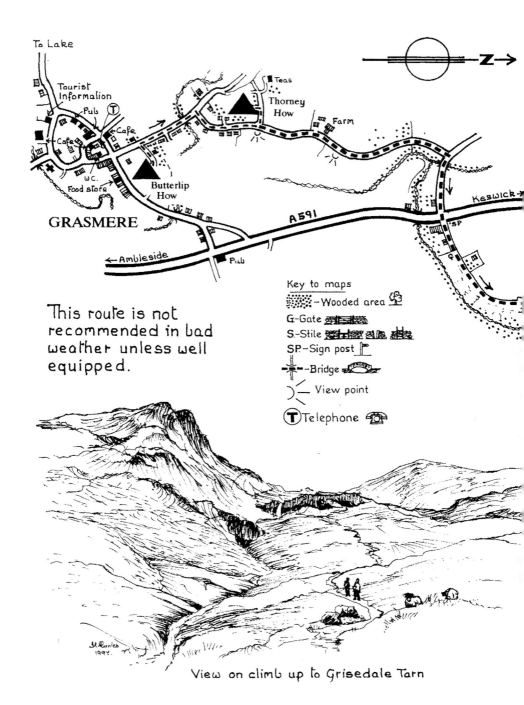

To Lake

Tourist Information

Pub (T)

Cafe

←Cafe

W.C.
Food store

GRASMERE

←Ambleside

Pub

Teas

Thorney How

Farm

Butterlip How

A591

Keswick→

SP

G

Z→

This route is not recommended in bad weather unless well equipped.

Key to maps

▦ -Wooded area 🌳
G-Gate ▦▦▦
S.-Stile ▦▦▦
SP-Sign post ⌐
✝- -Bridge ◠
)⌐— View point
(T)Telephone ☎

View on climb up to Grisedale Tarn

M. Davies 1994.

Walking route between
Grasmere YH and Patterdale YH: Map 1

see page 129

Approximate distances
Thorney How Hostel 8 miles, 12,75 Km.
Butterlip How Hostel 8.5 miles, 13,5 Km.

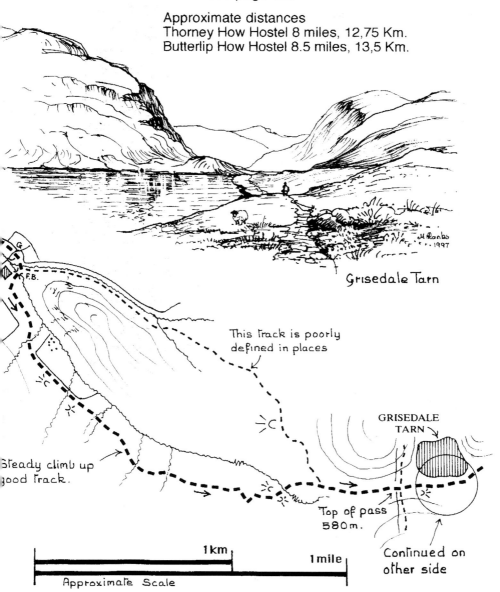

Grisedale Tarn

This track is poorly
defined in places

GRISEDALE
TARN

Steady climb up
good track.

Top of pass
580m.

Continued on
other side

1km

1mile

Approximate Scale

Walking route between
Grasmere YH and Patterdale YH: Map 2
see page 129

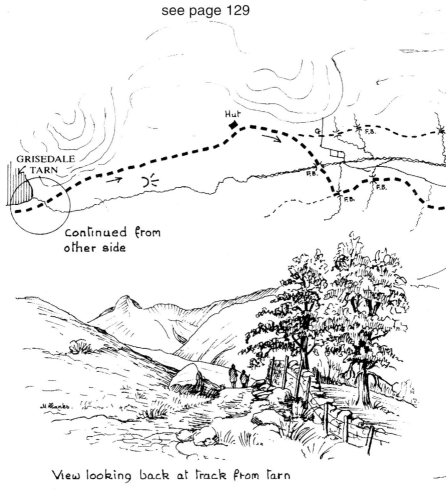

GRISEDALE TARN

Hut

F.B.

F.B.

F.B.

F.B.

continued from
other side

View looking back at track from tarn

1 km   1 mile

Approximate Scale

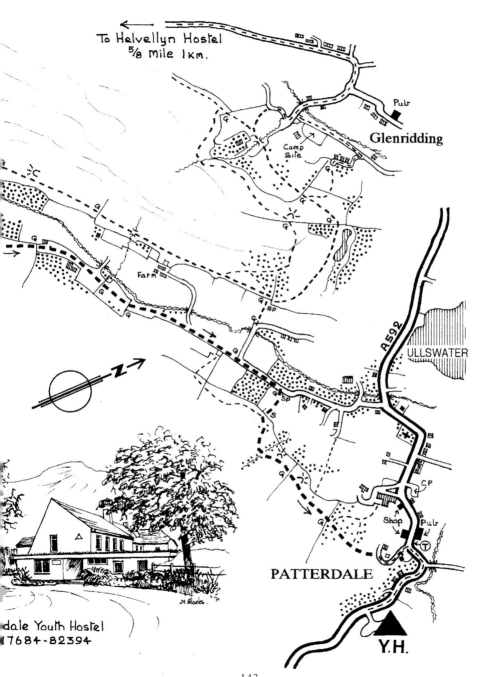

To Helvellyn Hostel
⅝ mile 1 km.

Glenridding

Pub

Camp Site

Farm

SP

A592

ULLSWATER

CP

Shop

Pub

T

PATTERDALE

...dale Youth Hostel
(7684·82394

Y.H.

Helvellyn YH to Patterdale YH

(The map is on pages 146/147)

The route to Patterdale crosses the valley upstream of the hostel and heads around the base of the fell to Grisedale. The direct route goes straight across the dale to a lane on the far side. It then climbs up behind Home Farm to reach Patterdale village close to the youth hostel. For a longer route, upon reaching Grisedale a path runs up the valley for about 2 miles (3.2km). The path crosses the dale at this point, returning down the far side.

Walks from Patterdale YH

(The map is on pages 148/149)

Crossing the valley from just below the hostel brings you to a path which runs up to Hartsop village. It continues along the valley past Brothers Water to the campsite at the rear of the Brotherswater Hotel. Here the path crosses the valley and returns back to Patterdale, initially by the lakeside. A detour from Hartsop can be taken up to Hayeswater. It lengthens the walk from 6.75 miles (10.75km) to 9.5 miles (15.25km). This reservoir drowned the village of Mardale.

Walks and steamer cruise from Patterdale YH

(The map is on pages 150/151)

This route has the novelty of starting with a cruise from Glenridding to Howtown. From the pier there are a choice of paths around Hallin Fell, the one along the lakeside being recommended. The majority of the route is fairly close to Ullswater. Being low level, it has the advantage of being suitable even in bad weather and only extends to 6 miles (9.6km). On the far side of Ullswater from the Howtown landing is Gowbarrow where Wordsworth and his sister Dorothy saw the daffodils 'fluttering and dancing'. They still grow there and are worth a springtime visit.

Kendal YH to Windermere YH and Ambleside YH

(The maps are on pages 152/155)

Take Underbarrow Road out of town and, having crossed the bypass, turn right into Gamblesmire Lane. The path crosses the fields to Underbarrow village before bearing northwest to head for Windermere, which takes five hours to reach. Here you can walk to the railway station where the YH bus from Ambleside meets the trains.

For Windermere YH, the route crosses the A591 and proceeds for another 3 miles (4.8km). At Common Farm, the road turns left and a path is taken which crosses the fields to the A592 close to the hostel. After crossing Trout Beck, it's a short walk along Bridge Lane. Troutbeck is seven hours from Kendal.

The route from Windermere YH to Ambleside YH is the reverse of the Ambleside YH to Windermere YH route described above.

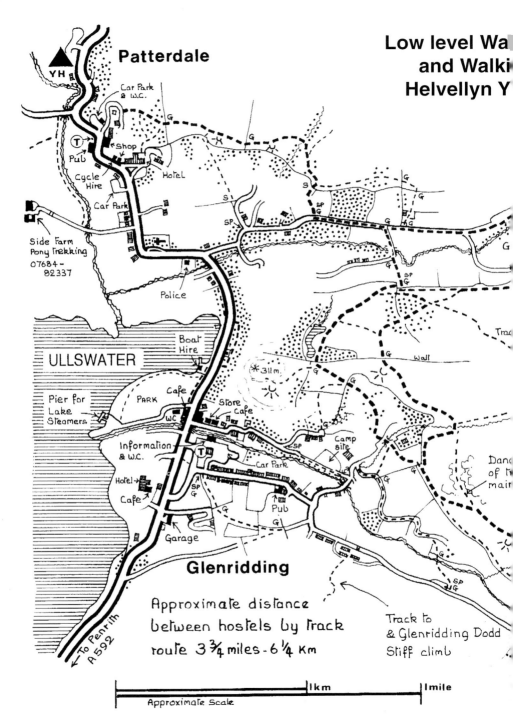

Patterdale

YH

Car Park & W.C.

T → Shop

Pub

Cycle Hire

Hotel

Car Park

Side Farm
Pony Trekking
07684-
82337

Police

ULLSWATER

Boat Hire

Pier for Lake Steamers

PARK

Cafe

WC

Store Cafe

Information & W.C.

T

Car Park

Hotel →

Cafe

Garage

Camp site

Pub

Glenridding

Approximate distance
between hostels by track
route 3¾ miles - 6¼ Km

To Penrith
A592

Track to
& Glenridding Dodd
Stiff climb

Wall

✱ 311m

Dan
of t
main

|——————————————————————|1km |1mile
Approximate Scale

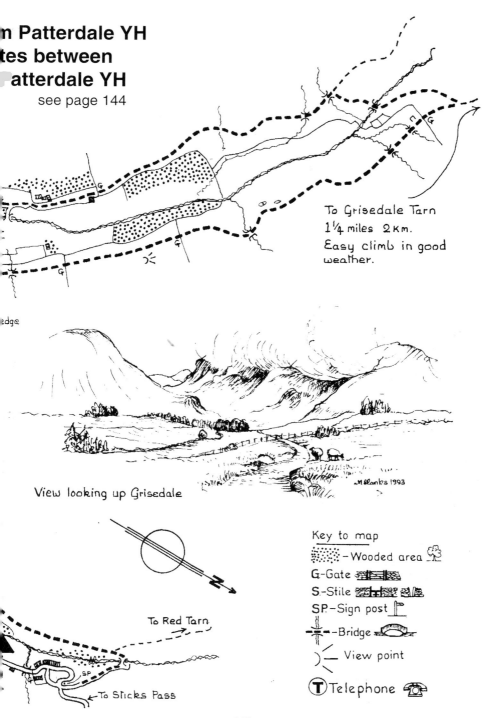

To Grisedale Tarn
1¼ miles 2 km.
Easy climb in good
weather.

edge

View looking up Grisedale

M Planks 1993

To Red Tarn

To Sticks Pass

SP

Key to map

- :::: – Wooded area
- G – Gate
- S – Stile
- SP – Sign post
- ╬ – Bridge
-)⌣ View point
- Ⓣ Telephone

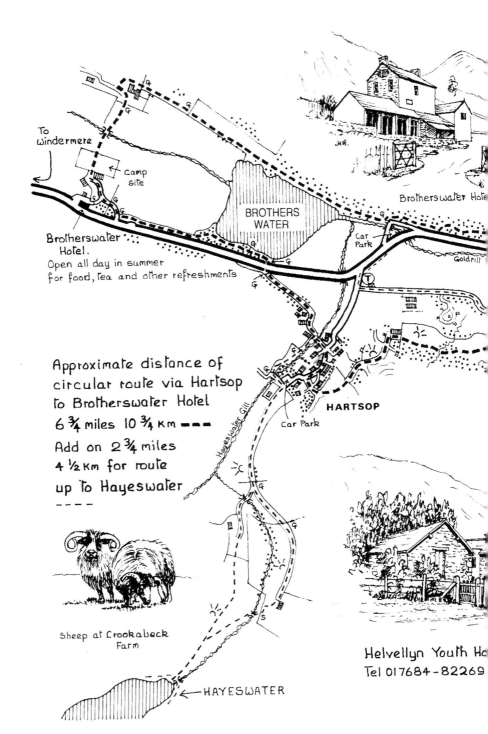

To Windermere

Camp Site

Brotherswater Hotel.
Open all day in summer
for food, tea and other refreshments

BROTHERS WATER

Brotherswater Hotel

Car Park

Goldrill

Approximate distance of
circular route via Hartsop
to Brotherswater Hotel
6 ¾ miles 10 ¾ km ▬ ▬ ▬
Add on 2 ¾ miles
4 ½ km for route
up to Hayeswater
▬ ▬ ▬ ▬

Hayeswater Gill

Car Park

HARTSOP

Sheep at Crookabeck
Farm

Helvellyn Youth Ho
Tel 017684-82269

HAYESWATER

148

Walks from Patterdale YH

see page 145

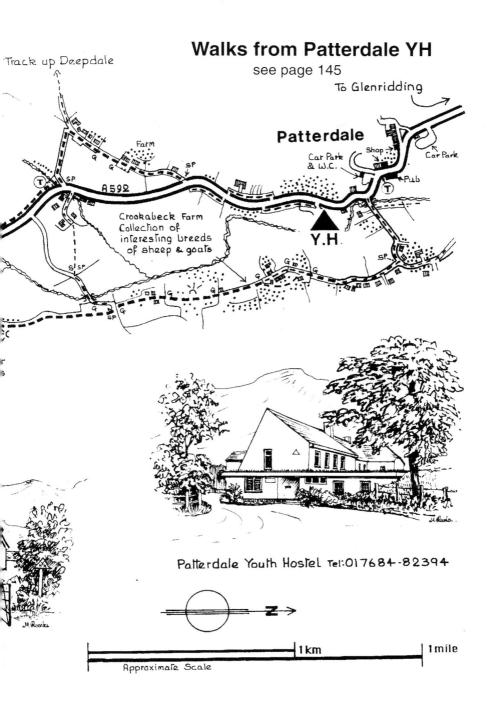

Patterdale Youth Hostel Tel:01768 4-82394

Approximate Scale

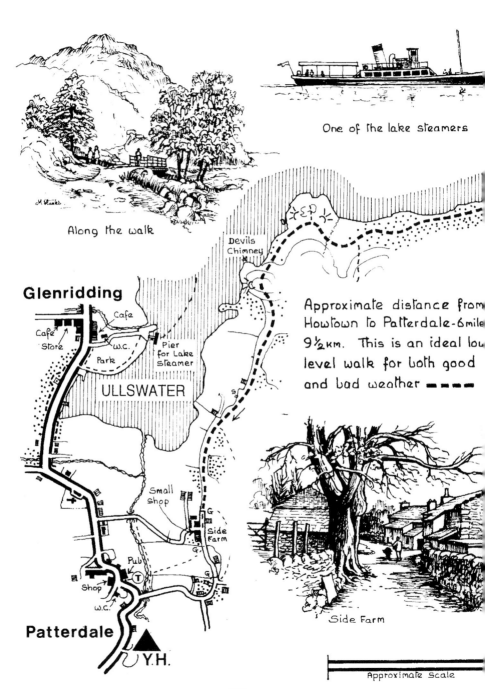

One of the lake steamers

Along the walk

Glenridding

Café
Café
Store
Park
W.C.
Pier for Lake Steamer

Devils Chimney

ULLSWATER

Approximate distance from Howtown to Patterdale - 6 miles 9½ km. This is an ideal low level walk for both good and bad weather ━ ━ ━

Small Shop

Side Farm

Pub

Shop

W.C.

Patterdale

Y.H.

Side Farm

Approximate Scale

Walks and Steamer Cruise from Patterdale YH

see page 145

View from Devils Chimney

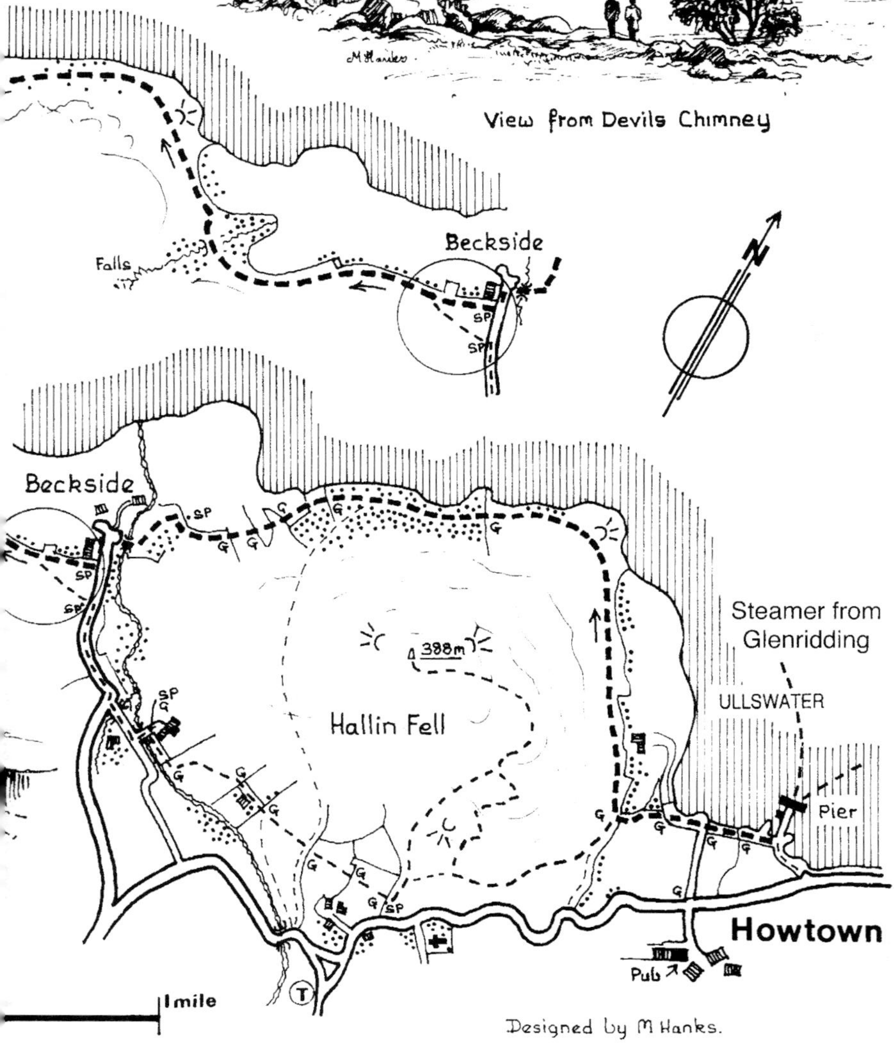

Falls

Beckside

SP
SP

Beckside

SP

SP

Steamer from
Glenridding

ULLSWATER

△ 388m

Hallin Fell

Pier

Howtown

Pub

1 mile

T

Designed by M Hanks.

151

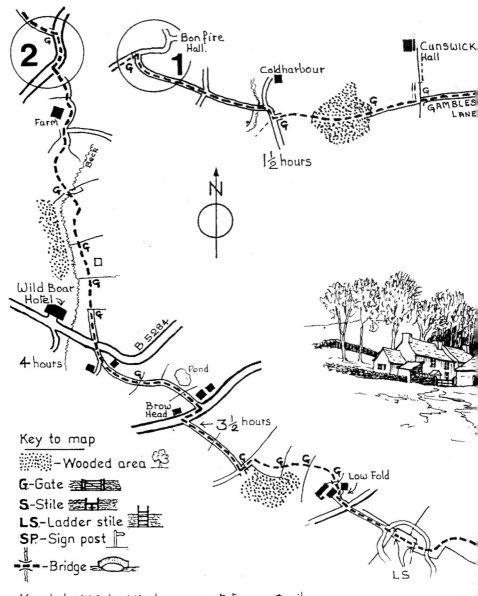

2 G

Bonfire Hall.

1 G

Coldharbour

Cunswick Hall

G

GAMBLES LANE

Farm

Beck

G

1½ hours

N

G

□

G

Wild Boar Hotel

G

B 5284

4 hours

Pond

G

Brow Head

← 3½ hours

S

S

G

G Low Fold

LS

Key to map
▨ –Wooded area 🌳

G-Gate

S-Stile

LS-Ladder stile

SP-Sign post

—‖— -Bridge

Kendal YHA to Windermere station — 9 miles
Windermere station to Windermere YHA – 3 miles
Windermere YHA to Ambleside YHA – 3½ miles

Approximate scale   1 KM   1 mile

Walking route between Kendal YH Windermere YH and Ambleside YH: Map 1

see page 145

G

G

SP

SP — G — Farm

To UNDERBARROW

BY-PASS

LS

G

G — LS

Quarry

Tarmac Office

Alternative route to avoid a dangerous stretch of road

Rifleman Arms Pub

Town Hall Tourist Office

Seat

HOSPITAL

Steps to door

Kendal

Brewery Art Centre

M.Planks

Low Fold
of the many farms on route

G — G
G

1

Bonfire Hall

Farm

G

Beck

G

SP — G

LS

S

S — G

SP

$2\frac{1}{4}$ hours

Broom Farm

UNDERBARROW

Kendal Youth Hostel

153

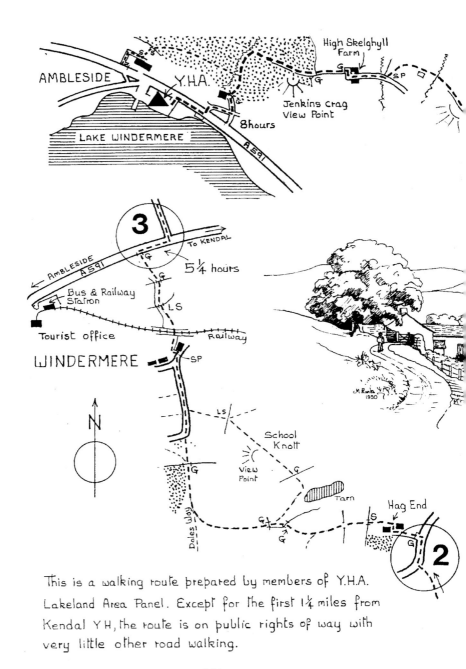

High Skelghyll Farm

AMBLESIDE Y.H.A.

Jenkins Crag View Point

8 hours

LAKE WINDERMERE

A 591

3

To KENDAL

AMBLESIDE A 591

5¼ hours

Bus & Railway Station

LS

Tourist office

Railway

WINDERMERE

SP

N

LS

School Knott

View Point

Tarn

Hag End

Doles Way

2

M. Parla. 1930

This is a walking route prepared by members of Y.H.A. Lakeland Area Panel. Except for the first 1¼ miles from Kendal Y.H., the route is on public rights of way with very little other road walking.

154

Walking route between Kendal YH.
Windermere YH and Ambleside YH: Map 2

see page 145

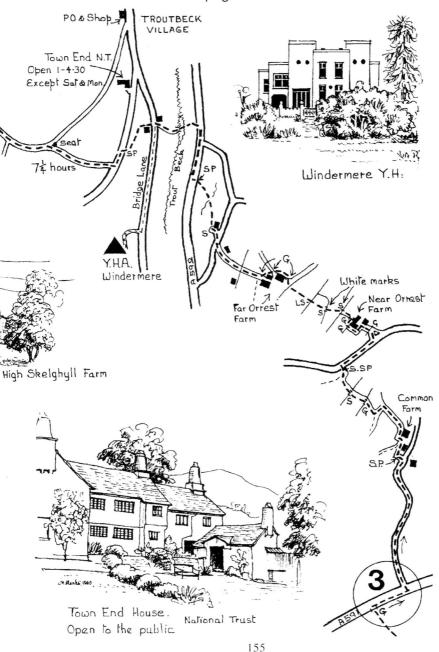

PO & Shop

TROUTBECK VILLAGE

Town End N.T.
Open 1-4.30
Except Sat & Mon.

Seat

7¼ hours

Bridge Lane

Trout Beck

SP

SP

S

A 592

Windermere Y.H.

Y.H.A.
Windermere

White marks

Near Orrest Farm

Far Orrest Farm

LS

S

S

G

G

G

S

High Skelghyll Farm

S.SP

S

G

Common Farm

S.P.

Town End House.
Open to the public

National Trust

3

A 59

G

155

Walks from Kendal YH

(The maps are on pages 158/161)

From the rear of the hostel one quickly reaches the golf course which is crossed on a path heading for the low lying Cunswick Fell and then to Hallhead Nab. Here there is a turn in direction as one heads eastwards to Burneside, a large village straddling the River Kent. Buses can be taken from Burneside to return to Kendal. Alternatively there is a riverside path which leads back into the middle of town.

A shorter route leaves town in a southwest direction along Brigsteer Road. After crossing the bridge over the A591, take the second signpost to the right. The path leads up onto the ridge path along Scout Scar. Turn north here along the ridge and cross Underbarrow Road by the mast. The path continues along Cunswick Fell before crossing the golf course to return to Kendal.

A longer route taking all day and covering nearly 10 miles (16km) also leaves town on Brigsteer Road and takes the path at the first signpost to the right beyond the A591. This climbs directly up onto the Scout Scar ridge. Turn south and, at the cairn, drop down off the ridge to the west. The path descends through woodland and then crosses the fields to Underbarrow village.

From the village a path goes north and then west heading for Gamblesmire Lane and Cunswick Fell. After walking north along the ridge for about half a mile, the path drops down to the golf course and returns to town. (See also **Kendal YH to Arnside YH** for route to Levens Hall).

Kendal YH to Arnside YH

(The maps are on pages 162/165)

From Kendal, the route follows the side of the River Kent for about 6 miles (9.6km). It passes Sedgwick Hall before reaching the deer park and Levens Hall. This Elizabethan house is open to the public. If you wish to visit the house, there is a bus either back to Kendal or on to Arnside (Cumberland 552, check the times and Sunday service before you leave).

The walk takes six hours to Arnside from Levens Hall. If you are not going to the hall, the path heads over the railway to follow the Lancaster to Kendal Canal before crossing the fields to Milnthorpe. Here it goes south through a deer park and past the Heron Corn Mill to reach Beetham. Turning right, Arnside is 2.25 hours away across the fields to the west.

Walks from Arnside YH

(The maps are on pages 166/169)

A path leaves Arnside along the River Kent estuary on an old railway line to Storth. It then heads inland around a large quarry to reach Milnthorpe. Here you can join the path described in the **Kendal YH to Arnside YH** route or return on the bus. To be safe, check bus times prior to leaving Arnside.

A second route climbs Arnside Knott to the south of the hostel before heading for Silverdale. The main path returns along the coast. The Silverdale Salt Marsh should be avoided because of a fast rising tide and quick-sands. A short distance from Silverdale is the Leighton Moss RSPB reserve, the only breeding ground in the north of England of the bittern.

Ask at the hostel for details of walks across Morecombe Bay with the official guide, who still walks the centuries-old route to the Lake District three times a week.
From the youth hostel, turn left and then right, cross the main road and go under the railway line. Cross the fields heading for Hazelslack. The path enters a wooded area thereafter and climbs up the Fairy Steps and then between rocks. It is way marked with blue arrows. Beetham is reached after 2.5 hours walking. Here the route goes northwards past the Heron Cornmill and through a deer park to Milnthorpe. The path then turns to the east to cross the fields to the Lancaster-Kendal Canal. The walk then turns north up the towpath.

Note the shorter route via Heversham which saves 4 miles (6.4km). A bus to Kendal can be boarded at Levens Bridge if you prefer (Cumberland 552, check the times and Sunday service before you leave). From Levens Bridge (where you can visit Levens Hall) the route to Kendal follows the side of the River Kent for about 6 miles (9.6km) to reach the town. This is a long route of 18 miles (29km) via Milton.

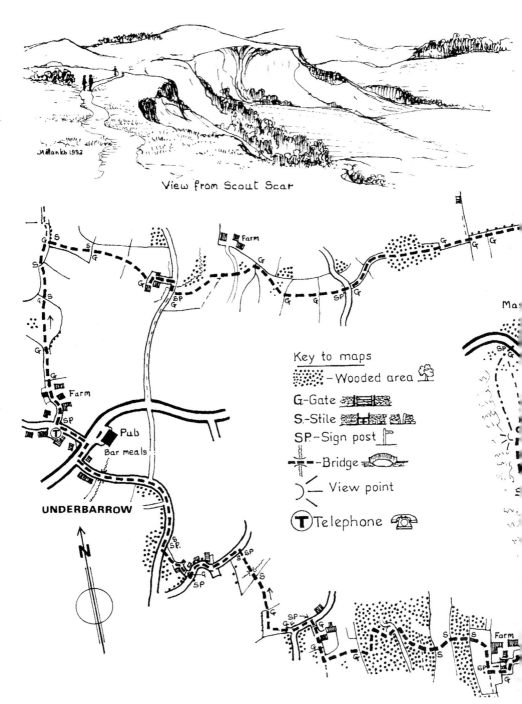

View from Scout Scar

M.Blanks 1993

Key to maps

▒ – Wooded area 🌳

G – Gate

S. – Stile

SP – Sign post

–╪– – Bridge

)– View point

Ⓣ Telephone ☎

Farm

Farm

Pub

Bar meals

UNDERBARROW

N

Farm

Walks from Kendal YH

see page 156

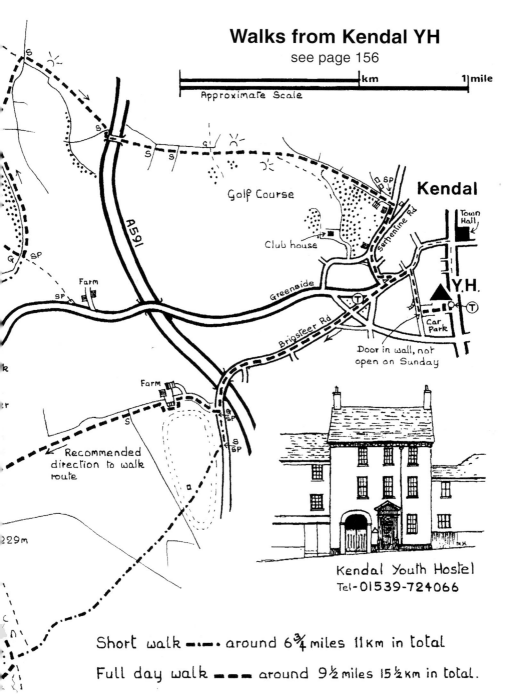

km   1 mile

Approximate Scale

Golf Course

Kendal

Club house

Town Hall

Farm

Greenside

Y.H.

Car Park

Brigsteer Rd

Door in wall, not open on Sunday

Farm

Recommended direction to walk route

229m

Kendal Youth Hostel
Tel-01539-724066

Short walk ——·—· around 6¾ miles 11 km in total

Full day walk ━━━ around 9½ miles 15½ km in total.

Walks from Kendal YH

see page 156

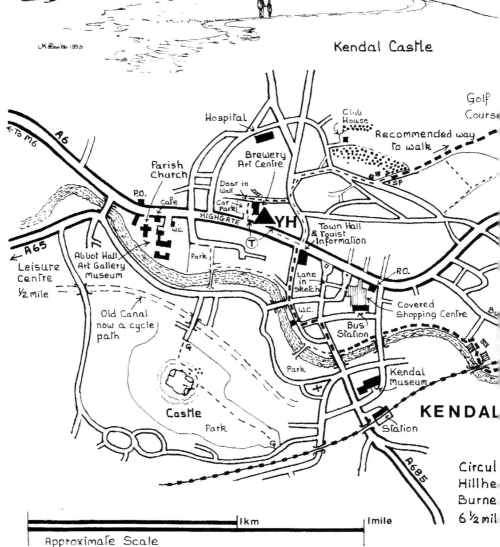

Kendal Castle

Walks from Kendal YH map showing roads and landmarks including: Golf Course, Club House, Recommended way to walk, Hospital, Brewery Art Centre, SP, To M6, A6, Parish Church, Door in Wall, Car Park, P.O., Cafe, HIGHGATE, W.C., YH, T, Town Hall & Tourist Information, A65, Leisure Centre ½ mile, Abbot Hall Art Gallery Museum, Park, Lane in sketch, P.O., Old Canal now a cycle path, W.C., Covered Shopping Centre, Bus Station, Park, Castle, Park, Kendal Museum, KENDAL, Station, A685, Circul Hillhe Burne 6½ mil

1km   1mile

Approximate Scale

cM Lambton 1993

160

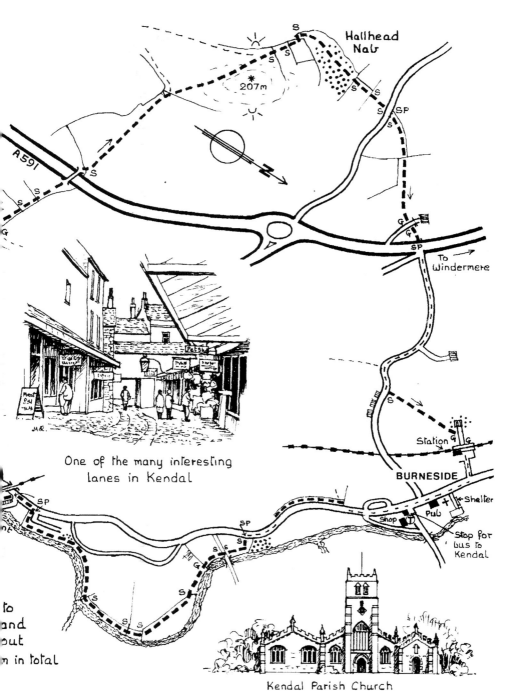

S
Hallhead
Nab
S
S
207m
SP
S

A591
S
S
S
G
G
G
SP
To
Windermere

One of the many interesting
lanes in Kendal

Station G G
BURNESIDE
Shelter
Shop
Pub
Stop for
bus to
Kendal

SP
SP
SP
G
to
and
out
m in total
S

Kendal Parish Church

Walking route between
Arnside YH and Kendal YH: Map 1
see page 157

Arnside Youth Hostel Tel. 0524-

Key to map

▓▓▓ – Wooded area 🌳

G-Gate ▦

S.-Stile ▦

SP.-Sign post ⚑

⬕ -Bridge 🌉

Distance via Milton 18 miles **28** km **9½ hours walk.**
via Heversham 14 miles **23** km – – –
to Milnthorpe 5 miles **8** km
Levens 7½ miles **12** km

Buses run between Mil
Levens bridge and Kenc
every hour except on S

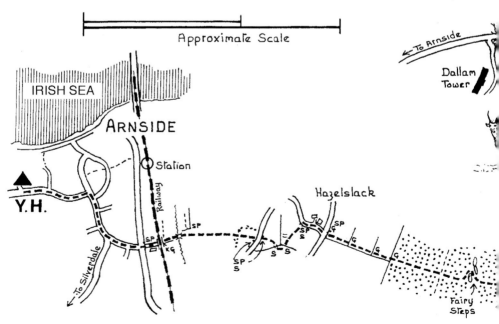

Approximate Scale

IRISH SEA

ARNSIDE

Station

Railway

Y.H.

To Silverdale

To Arnside

Dallam Tower

Hazelslack

SP

Fairy Steps

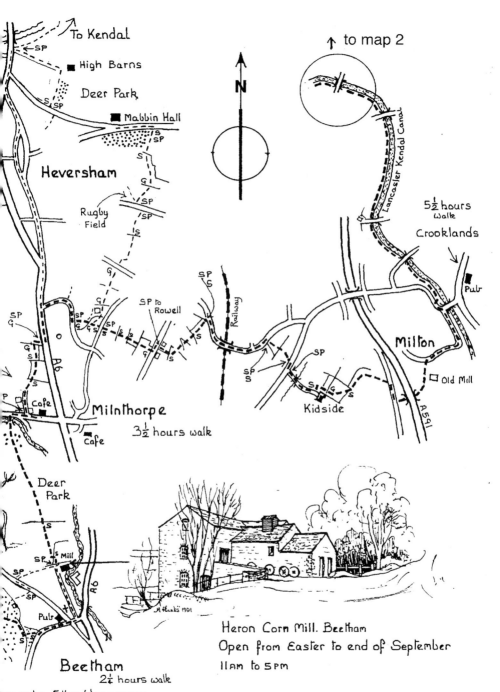

To Kendal

High Barns

Deer Park

Mabbin Hall

↑ to map 2

N

Lancaster Kendal Canal

5½ hours walk

Crooklands

Pub

Heversham

Rugby Field

SP to Rowell

Railway

Milton

Old Mill

SP

SP

SP

Kidside

Milnthorpe

3½ hours walk

Cafe

Cafe

Deer Park

Mill

Pub

Beetham

2¼ hours walk

en rocks - Follow blue arrows.

Heron Corn Mill. Beetham
Open from Easter to end of September
11am to 5pm

M Hanks 1991

163

Walking route between
Arnside YH and Kendal YH: Map 2

see page 157

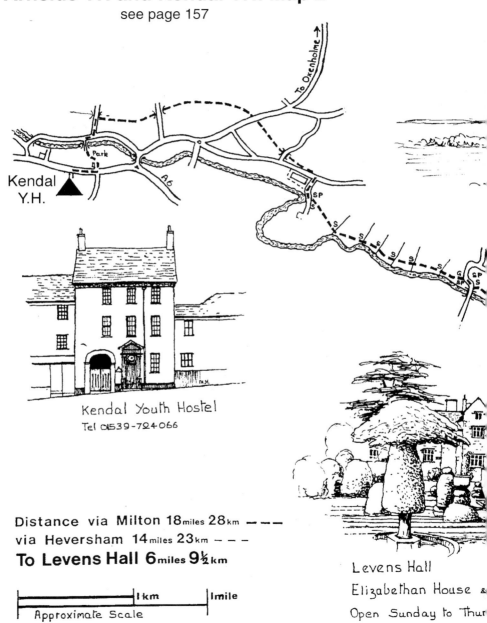

Kendal
Y.H.

To Oxenholme →

Park

A6

SP

Kendal Youth Hostel
Tel 0539-724066

Distance via Milton 18 miles 28 km — — —
via Heversham 14 miles 23 km — — —
To Levens Hall 6 miles 9½ km

1 km   1 mile

Approximate Scale

Levens Hall
Elizabethan House &
Open Sunday to Thur

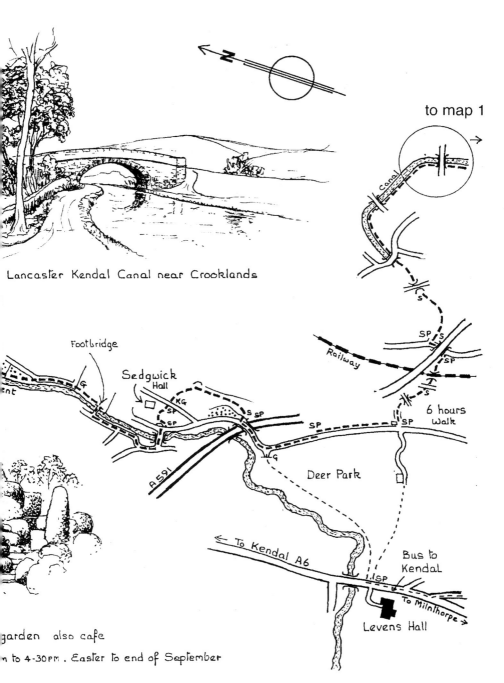

Lancaster Kendal Canal near Crooklands

to map 1

Footbridge

Sedgwick Hall

Railway

6 hours Walk

Deer Park

A591

← To Kendal A6

Bus to Kendal

To Milnthorpe →

Levens Hall

garden also cafe

to 4-30pm. Easter to end of September

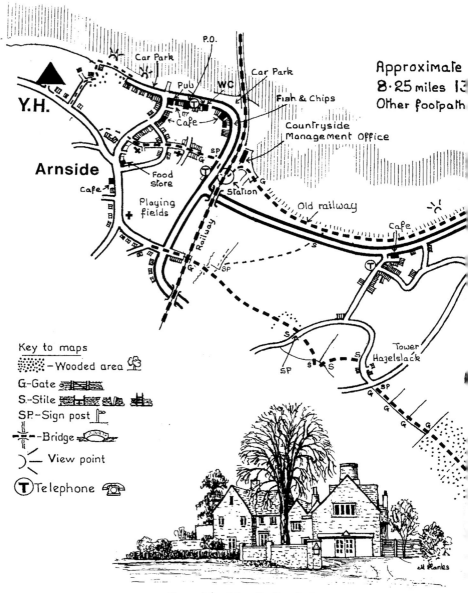

P.O.

Car Park

Car Park

Pub

WC

Fish & Chips

Cafe

Countryside
Management Office

Y.H.

Approximate
8·25 miles 13
Other footpath

SP

G

Arnside

Cafe

Food
Store

Playing
fields

Station

Railway

SP

G

Old railway

S

Cafe

T

Tower
Hazelslack

S

SP

S

S

SP

G

G

G

SP

G

G

Key to maps

- Wooded area
- G—Gate
- S.—Stile
- SP—Sign post
- —Bridge
-)(— View point
- (T) Telephone

Arnside Youth Hostel Tel: 01524-761781

1km

1mile

Approximate Scale

Walks from Arnside YH

see page 157

e of main walk

- - - -

Farm at Hazelslack

Pub

P.O.

SP
S

Quarry

Haverbrack

Dallam Tower

SP
S

SP

Buses to Arnside from Milnthorpe

Check with warden for up to date timetable

Cafe

To Kendal →

WC

Cafe

Bus Stop

MILNTHORPE

Deer Park

A6

ry Steps

SP
S

Mill

SP

SP

BEETHAM

P.O.

een rocks
arrows

S   S

Pub

Heron Corn Mill Beetham

Open from Easter to end of September
11am to 5pm

To Lancaster

167

Walks from Arnside YH

see page 157

The Pepper Pot above Silverdale

Arnside

Silverdale Salt

Beware of fast rising tide

Jack Scout

Lindeth Tower

Wolf House Craft Gallery & Cafe

Garden Centre

Jenny Brown Point

Chimney

Wood Hall

Pub

P.O.

Pub

WC

Hazelwood

Food Store

SILVERDALE

The P.
This obelis
to commem
of Queen

← To Carnforth

Evens Wood

Leighton Moss
R S P B reserve & Cafe

Golf Course

Car Park

Garden Centre

Station

For times of trains
to Arnside. Check
with warden

Chimney at Jenny Browns Point

Approximate distance of main circular
route 8 miles 13km in total

White Creek

Caravan Park

Farm

sands

Caravan Park

Hollins Farm Tens

New Barns Bay

C.P.

IRISH SEA

Arnside Knott
521ft

YH

Arnside

ted Jubilee

Farm

Redhills wood

Cafe

Cafe

Car Park

Quarry

Arnside Tower Ruin
This is a medieval
Pele Tower

Cafe

Food Store

Pub

P.O.

WC

C.P.

Pub

Playing Fields

Railway

B5282

Station

Countryside management office

1km

1mile

Approximate scale

169

LANDMARK VISITORS GUIDES

* **Practical guides for the independent traveller**

* **Written in the form of touring itineraries**

* **Full colour illustrations and maps**

* **Detailed Landmark FactFile of practical information**

* **Landmark Visitors Guides highlight all the interesting places you will want to see, so ensuring that you make the most of your visit**

AVAILABLE SHORTLY:

1. Britain

Cornwall	Cotswolds & Shakespeare Country
Devon	Edinburgh
Jersey	Lake District
Peak District	Scotland
Somerset, Dorset & Wilts	Yorkshire Dales
Guernsey	Hampshire

2. Europe

Bruges	Black Forest
Alps and Jura	Provence
Italian Lakes	Gran Canaria
Norway	

3. Other

India: Goa	Bangkok and Phuket
India: Kerala and The South	Thailand
New Zealand	

LANDMARK
Publishing Ltd ● ● ●

Waterloo House, 12 Compton, Ashbourne, Derbyshire DE6 1DA England

THE YOUTH HOSTELS

Ambleside YH

Waterhead, Ambleside, Cumbria, LA22 0EU
Tel: 015394 32304   Fax: 015394 34408

Accommodation details:

Thirty six 2-5 bedded rooms and sixteen 6-8 bedded rooms. Open daily, all year around.
Daytime access to lounge, TV room, games room, drying room etc. The coffee shop is
open all day to the general public. Dinner is served 17.30 - 19.30 and a table licence is
available for those taking dinner.

Getting there:

From Spring to Autumn, the YHA operates a shuttle bus from Windermere railway station
until early evening. Free transport to Ambleside.
By bus: Stagecoach Cumberland services from the surrounding areas, Tel: 01946 63222.
The YHA Centre is on the A 591 Windermere to Ambleside road, on the left just beyond
the Esso station as you approach Ambleside.

Description:

This is a large YHA Centre. It used to be three hotels which were merged into one before
the YHA purchased it in 1972. It has recently been extensively refurbished and is a
flagship for the YHA. It offers a high standard of comfort, with many small family rooms,
some of them overlooking Lake Windermere. This is possibly the best youth hostel in
Europe in terms of comfort, facilities and position. It has its own jetty and launching area
and is only a few yards from the steamer jetty for trips down the lake. The lawns extend
down to the water and there are plenty of seats and picnic tables for your use.

Arnside YH

Oakfield Lodge, Redhills Road, Arnside, Carnforth, Lancashire LA5 0AT
Tel: 01524 761781 Fax: 01524 762589

Accommodation details:

A variety of large and small rooms are available. Open throughout the year except for certain winter periods. The building is fully open from 17.00 but daytime access is available to the games room, toilets, drying room, self-catering kitchen etc. Dinner is served at 19.00.

Getting there:

From the South leave the M6 at Junction 35, take the A6 to Milnthorpe. From the North leave M6 at Junction 36, take the A65 and B6385 to Milnthorpe. Take the B5282 to Arnside. Turn right at the T-junction, and follow the main road through the village to the YHA sign on the right (Redhills Road).
By bus: Stagecoach Cumberland 552 from Cumberland.

Description:

Originally built for a wealthy Edwardian doctor, this mellow Tudor-style house has spent much of its history as a girls boarding school. Set in a commanding position above the River Kent estuary, it has stunning views across the water to the southern fells of the Lake District. The YH is equipped to a high standard and offers comfortable accommodation for families, groups and individuals wishing to explore this less crowded area. The headmistress' study and drawing room are now the two sitting rooms, and most of the bedrooms are suitable for families. The dining room looks out over the terrace, a pleasant place from which to relax and watch the sunset on summer evenings.

Black Sail

Black Sail Hut, Ennerdale, Cleator, Cumbria CA23 3AY
No telephone

Accommodation details:

Dormitory accommodation in three bedrooms. Basic facilities only. Open March to October. Usually closed one night in the week (Sunday or Monday). Opens 17.00 but a toilet and shelter is available if you arrive early.

Getting there:

This hostel may only be reached on foot. The bus may be taken from Keswick to Seatoller (Stagecoach Cumberland 79). It's a 3.5 miles (4.8km) hike from Seatoller and uphill most of the way!

Description:

A former bothy remotely situated at the head of Ennerdale and surrounded by stunning scenery, it used to be occupied during the sheep shearing season to house the shepherd. It has a cosy atmosphere and cooked meals may be purchased (at 19.00). Because of the isolated position there is no electricity and no heating in the bedrooms. Facilities include sitting room, self catering kitchen and shower.

Borrowdale YH

Longthwaite, Borrowdale, Keswick, Cumbria CA12 5XE
Tel: 017687 77257 Fax: 017687 77393

Accommodation details:

Extensively refurbished in 1996, all bedrooms have wash basins and bunk lights. Fully open from 13.00, dinner is served at 19.00. Mostly small family-sized rooms. There are travel cots, high chairs and a toy corner available for very young guests.

Getting there:

Follow 'Borrowdale' signs from Keswick, turn second right after Rosthwaite village to the end of the lane.
By bus: Stagecoach Cumberland 79 from Keswick

Description:

A purpose built youth hostel constructed mainly of Canadian red cedar. Open for most of the year (closes first few weeks of year) and shut Monday and Tuesday up to Easter.

Buttermere YH

Buttermere, Cockermouth, Cumbria CA13 9XA
Tel: 017687 70245 Fax: 017687 70231

Accommodation details:

Mostly small rooms ideal for families. Open from 17.00 but daytime access to drying room, self catering kitchen and information area. Dinner served 19.00.

Getting there:

A quarter of a mile out of Buttermere village on road to Honister Pass and Borrowdale on B5289.
By bus: Stagecoach Cumberland 77 from Keswick (May-October only).

Description:

A former hotel converted to a youth hostel with financial assistance from the King George VI fund in memory of the late king. The hostel stands on a rise overlooking Buttermere Lake. It is open all year (except closed for Sunday and/or Monday between September and March, but open daily over New Year period).

Carrock Fell YH

High Row Cottage, Haltcliffe, Hesket Newmarket, Wigton, Cumbria CA7 8JT
Tel/fax: 016974 78325

Accommodation details:

A small traditional youth hostel with three dormitories. In the winter only open on the 'rent a hostel' scheme. From Easter to the end of October, open except for Mondays and at certain times also Tuesdays. Opens at 17.00 and dinner served at 19.00.

Getting there:

Three miles (4.8km) north of Mungrisdale at High Row. Turn right off Mungrisdale to Caldbeck Road. The hostel is the first house up the track on the left.
By bus: The Penrith - Wigton bus passes to within 2.5 miles.

Description:

This eighteenth century farmhouse retains many of its original features including stone floors and old beams. It only has capacity for 20 people. The conversion work has been done in a very sensitive manner and has resulted in a pleasant ambience which has made Carrock Fell YH very popular. It is situated in a peaceful hamlet on the edge of the Caldbeck Fells.

Cockermouth YH

Double Mills, Cockermouth, Cumbria CA13 0DS
Tel: 01900 822561 Fax: 01900 822561

Accommodation details:

Another traditional youth hostel with three bedrooms accommodating a maximum of 28 people. In the winter, only open on the 'rent a hostel' scheme. From Easter to the end of October, open except for Wednesdays and at certain times also Tuesdays. Opens at 17.00 and dinner served at 19.00.

Getting there:

From Main Street follow Station Street and then turn left into Fern Bank. Take the track at the end of Fern Bank. From the A66 take the A5086 to Cockermouth then the 2nd right into Fern Bank. Approach down track off Fern Bank.
By bus: Stagecoach Cumberland X5 BR.

Description:

A seventeenth century watermill, complete with its waterwheel and some of its old grinding stones. Situated on the banks of the River Cocker, ten minutes from the town centre.

Coniston Coppermines YH

Coniston, Cumbria LA21 8HP
Tel/fax: 015394 41261

Accommodation details:

Another three-bedroomed traditional youth hostel. Open on the 'rent a hostel' scheme only, between November and mid-March. At other times closed Wednesday/Thursday except during June, July and August when it is open daily. Opening time is at 17.00 but from 13.00 the lounge, kitchen, showers and wc are available. Dinner is served at 19.00.

Getting there:

From the main road through Coniston (the A593 or Yewdale Road) take the small road that lies between the Black Bull pub and the Co-op, and follow it for 1.25 miles (2km) to the hostel. The road soon becomes a track.
By bus: There is a service from Ambleside and Hawkshead to Coniston village.
By rail: Trains run to Windermere Station, and a regular bus service runs to Ambleside, where you can get a connection to Coniston.

Description:

This building used to be the manager's house and office of a former copper mine. The building dates from the 1830s and was one of the first youth hostels in the Lakes. It has recently been refurbished.

Coniston Holly How YH

Holly How, Far End, Coniston, Cumbria LA21 8DD
Tel: 015394 41323 Fax: 015394 41803

Accommodation details:

A mixture of dormitories and small family rooms. The hostel accommodates a maximum of 60 guests. Open Friday, Saturday and Sunday for most of the year and rest of the week in July, August and part of September, part of spring and all school holidays. Reception opens 17.00 and dinner is served at 19.00. There is daytime access to the lounge, toilets, drying room and self-catering kitchen.

Getting there:

Just north of Coniston, off the main A593 road to Ambleside.
By bus: There is a service from Ambleside and Hawkshead to Coniston village.
By rail: Trains run to Windermere station, and a regular bus service runs to Ambleside where you can get a connection to Coniston.

Description:

A traditional slate built former guest house with a large attractive garden. It is situated close to the town centre and is conveniently sited for walks to Tarn Hows (one of the most beautiful places in Lakeland) and Coniston Water, where you can explore the lake on the beautifully restored steam yacht 'Gondola'.

Derwentwater YH

Barrow House, Borrowdale, Keswick, Cumbria CA12 5UR
Tel: 017687 77246 Fax: 017687 77396

Accommodation details:

Mostly 5-8 bedded rooms, some family rooms. Open daily from 13.00. Dinner at 19.00. Self catering kitchen. Table licence available for those taking dinner. This youth hostel closes end November-December. Otherwise open all year round.

Getting there:

The centre is 2 miles (3.2km) south of Keswick on the Borrowdale road. The concealed drive entrance is 100m past left turn to Ashness Bridge and Watendlath.
By Bus: Stagecoach Cumberland 79 (Keswick-Seatoller) Tel: 01946 63222
By Boat: from Keswick
By Train: from Penrith Station - 34/5 bus; from Lancaster Station; 555 bus (goes past Windermere Station) Tel: 01228 812812.

Description:

Barrow House is a large 200 year old mansion built by Mr Pocklington, a Nottingham mill owner. It is set in 15 acres (6 hectares) of grounds overlooking Derwentwater. Derwentwater was one of YHA's earliest hostels, but was sold. Fortunately it was later repurchased.
Because of work by John Adam, the famous eighteenth century architect - the most outstanding example being the first floor Adam Room with its splendid fireplace - the building is protected. In the garden is a 108ft (33m) waterfall. The stream flows under Ashness Bridge at the rear of the building. The view of Derwentwater from the bridge is one of the most photographed scenes in the Lakes.

Elterwater YH

Elterwater, Ambleside, Cumbria LA22 9HX
Tel: 015394 37245 Fax: 015394 37120

Accommodation details:

An old farmhouse and barn offering small rooms and dormitories. Opens daily in March but also open Friday and Saturday only from Mid-February. In October not open Mondays. In November and December (pre Christmas) closed Sunday and Monday. Hostel opens 17.00 but public rooms available during the day. Dinner served 19.00.

Getting there:

Leave Ambleside on the A593 and follow signs for Coniston. After about 2 miles (3.2km), turn right onto the B5343, signposted to Langdale. After 2 miles, turn left — signposted Elterwater. After a quarter of a mile you will enter the village. Cross the bridge over the river. The youth hostel is 200 yards along on the right — the last building in the village. By bus: Stagecoach Cumberland 516 from Ambleside.

Description:

Situated on the edge of one of Lakeland's most attractive villages near the impressive Langdale Pikes. Nearby on Elterwater Common, the Barnhowe Handspinning Centre may be visited where you can learn to spin wool.

Ennerdale YH

Cat Crag, Ennerdale, Cleator, Cumbria CA23 3AX
Tel: 01946 861237

Accommodation details:

Two former forest cottages situated about a mile above Ennerdale lake. Only open on the 'rent a hostel' scheme in winter. From Easter to the end of October it is open daily except Tuesdays (and Wednesdays out of main season). Opens at 17.00 and dinner served at 19.00.

Getting there:

Stagecoach Cumberland from Keswick (May-October only). Alight at Buttermere. Hostel is three miles away over fell. Alternatively Bus No 17 from Whitehaven, alighting at Kirkland, seven miles away; or Bus 79 from Keswick to Seatoller, which is also seven miles away (follow hostel route from Borrowdale to Honister, and then the hostel route from Ennerdale to Black Sail and Black Sail to Honister Hause in reverse.

Description:

This small hostel provides comfortable centrally heated accommodation for 24 guests in four or six bedded rooms. It is heated and lit by calorgas having no electricity. If the weather is cold or wet, the hostel's common room and drying rooms are usually open during the afternoons.

Eskdale YH

Boot, Holmrook, Cumbria CA19 1TH
Tel: 019467 23219 Fax: 019467 23163

Accommodation details:

A purpose built youth hostel, set back from the busy valley road. It has six 2-6 bedded family rooms plus three larger dormitories. Open daily from 17.00, with lounge, drying room, toilets and laundry available from 13.00. Dinner is served at 19.00.

Getting there:

Public transport is limited, Dalegarth Station on the Ravensglass - Eskdale steam railway is 1.5 miles away. The road to Eskdale over the Wrynose and Hard Knott passes is narrow and not suitable to coaches. It is also impassable in icy conditions (Hard Knott Pass has a 1:3 gradient in places). The alternative route is via Broughton-in-Furness.

Description:

This hostel was built in the early 1950's. It has recently been refurbished and now has a relaxed and comfortable atmosphere. It is ideally situated for exploring a peaceful and beautiful part of the Lakes.

Grasmere (Butterlip How) YH

Butterlip How, Easedale Road, Grasmere, Ambleside, Cumbria LA22 9QG
Tel: 015394 35316 Fax: 015394 35798

Accommodation details:

A traditional Lakeland slate Victorian country house, set in its own extensive grounds on the edge of the village.
Open: Most of the year, but usually closed November and most of December. Also closed on Mondays out of season. The hostel is open from 13.00. There are several small family bedrooms each with wash basin. The annexe (now known as How Lodge), has been refurbished and has 26 beds in 2 and 4 bedded rooms all with wash hand basins and adequate toilet and shower facilities. These rooms are available with daytime access.

Getting there:

Leave the village via Easedale Road. The hostel drive is on your right about 400 yards up the road.
By bus: Stagecoach Cumberland 555 (Lancaster-Keswick) and the 599 from Windermere.

Description:

Grasmere YH (Butterlip How) together with the surrounding land was originally a farm. Over the years it has been added to quite extensively. This can be seen when looking down onto the building from Butterlip How, noting all the different roof shapes and angles. For some time the building was then used as a a private residence before becoming a hotel after World War II. In 1952 it was taken over by the YHA.

Grasmere is one of the most popular villages of Lakeland. William Wordsworth lived in the village and his homes at Dove Cottage and nearby Rydal Mount are open to the public. He lies buried in Grasmere churchyard. Rowing boats may be hired on Grasmere Lake.

Grasmere (Thorney How) YH

Thorney How, Grasmere, Cumbria LA22 9QW
Tel: 015394 35591 Fax: 015394 35866

Accommodation details:

This is the first building to be owned by the YHA. It is fully open from Easter to the end of September and open for most of the rest of the year except Tuesdays and Wednesdays. The hostel was refurbished a few years ago and has several small family rooms. Reception opens daily at 17.00, with daytime access to most rooms except bedrooms. Dinner served at 19.00.

Getting there:

Turn up Easedale Road in the village centre close to the Heaton Cooper Gallery.
By bus: Stagecoach Cumberland 555 (Lancaster-Keswick) and the 599 from Windermere (alight in Grasmere).

Description:

A former farmhouse, with parts of the building over 300 years old. Despite extensions, it still retains its original charm and atmosphere. Grasmere is one of the most popular villages in the Lake District.

Hawkshead YH

Esthwaite Lodge, Hawkshead, Ambleside, Cumbria LA22 0QD
Tel: 015394 36293 Fax: 015394 36720

Accommodation details:

A Regency mansion and Coach House family annexe overlooking Esthwaite Water. This is a large youth hostel accommodating 115 people with lots of small rooms. Open all year except for a few weeks in mid-winter. Closed Sunday/Monday during the winter season. Open from 13.00. Dinner at 19.00. The hostel has a table licence.

Getting there:

Take the Newby Bridge Road out of Hawkshead village, down the west side of the lake.
By bus: Stagecoach Cumberland 505/6 from Ambleside.

Description:

Esthwaite Lodge was the home of Francis Brett Young and there is a library of his books at the hostel. The building has some superb Regency features such as its elegant staircase and various ceilings. The YHA has invested significant capital in refurbishing the hostel. The Coach House and stables have been converted to ten family rooms, some with ensuite facilities. All have keys and are accessible throughout the day. Travel cots and a high chair are on hand for small children.

Helvellyn YH

Greenside, Glenridding, Penrith, Cumbria CA11 0QR
Tel/fax: 017684 82269

Accommodation details:

An isolated and peaceful youth hostel 1.5 miles (2.4km) from Glenridding near the shore of Ullswater. Open for most of the year, although restricted winter opening times and closed Sundays from Easter to the end of June. Reception opens 17.00, sitting area and toilets open from 1pm. Dinner served 19.00.

Getting there:

Signposted from Glenridding. The lane to the hostel is unsurfaced for last 3/4 mile. Bus from Penrith stops in village (CMS 108).

Description:

A traditional lakeland stone building which was formally Greenside Mine manager's house. Ideal stepping off point for Helvellyn and surrounding peaks. All small bedrooms.

Honister Hause YH

Honister Hause, Seatoller, Keswick, Cumbria CA12 5XN
Tel: 017687 77267

Accommodation details:

Set in a spectacular setting beside the road on the summit of Honister Pass at 1200ft above sea level. Open from spring to end of October, closed Wednesday and Thursday evenings prior to the end of May and in September and October. Reception opens 17.00, with a wet-weather shelter available before that. Dinner served at 19.00.

Getting there:

Situated on the Keswick-Buttermere Road (B5289).
By bus: Stagecoach Cumberland 79 from Keswick to Seatoller (then 1.5 mile, 2.4km walk up to summit of Honister Pass). Additional peak-season bus No 77/77A.

Description:

Originally a wooden barracks for slate miners, it opened in 1942 but was replaced by the current, comfortable accommodation in 1960. Although very isolated, it generates its own electricity and is centrally heated. The hostel has beds for 30 people in all, with some small bedrooms available. The altitude of the hostel is very convenient for high level walks in central Lakeland.

Kendal YH

118 Highgate, Kendal, Cumbria LA9 4HE
Tel: 01539 724066 Fax: 01539 724906

Accommodation details:

Opened in 1987 by Princess Anne. The hostel is open for most of the year, although likely to be shut Sundays and Mondays out of season. Open daily at 17.00. Dinner served at 19.00.

Getting there:

Kendal YH is only 7 miles (11.2km) from junction 36 of the M6. There is parking in the Brewery car park at the rear.
By bus: Numerous bus services pass through or start/end in Kendal.
By rail: Oxenholme main line station is 1.5 miles (2.4km) away, with a branch line calling at Kendal Station (1mile, 1.6km from the hostel).

Description:

A Georgian townhouse situated in the main street. It forms part of the Brewery Arts Centre which has regular festivals including folk music each August and Jazz and Blues in October/November (full details available from the youth hostel). Plenty of small rooms, each with wash basin and adjacent to showers and toilets.

Keswick YH

Station Road, Keswick, Cumbria CA12 5LH
Tel: 017687 72484 Fax: 017687 74129

Accommodation details:

Situated adjacent to the Greta River with a walkway above the water! Open virtually all year. Reception open all day. Fully open from 13.00. Dinner served at 19.00.

Getting there:

Follow 'Leisure Pool' signs into Station Road. Turn left onto walkway upon reaching river.
By bus: various services to Keswick; Stagecoach Cumberland X5; Wrights 888 (from Penrith Railway Station); 34/5 from Whitehaven (passes Workington Station); 555 from Lancaster (passes Windermere Station).

Description:

An excellent base for exploring Skiddaw, Blencathra and the Derwentwater area, this former temperance hotel offers mainly small rooms, with full central heating and superb views from its sitting rooms and balcony across Fitz Park to Skiddaw.

Langdale YH

High Close, Loughrigg, Ambleside, Cumbria LA22 9HJ
Tel: 015394 37313 Fax: 015394 37101

Accommodation details:

A lovely house known as High Close, owned by the National Trust and situated between Grasmere and Elterwater. Restricted opening in winter; open daily from Easter to end of August. Open daily except Sunday from mid-February to Easter and in September and October. Reception opens 17.00 but wet-weather shelter open during the day. Dinner served at 18.30.

Getting there:

From Ambleside take the A593 (to Coniston and Langdale). After 1.5 miles (2.4km) turn right (before reaching Skelwith Bridge) and follow minor road uphill for 1.75 miles (2.8km). At summit of Red Bank, turn left and High Close is 1/4 mile on the left.
By bus: Stagecoach Cumberland 516 from Ambleside. Alight 3/4 mile before Elterwater, then a 3/4 mile walk. Alternatively take bus to Grasmere and walk from there 1.5 miles (2.4km).

Description:

A large Victorian mansion, part of it dating back to the seventeenth century and extended several times since. It has superb gardens which are open to the public. Although a large youth hostel, it has seven family rooms — the rest are in dormitory rooms.

Patterdale YH

Goldrill House, Patterdale, Penrith, Cumbria CA11 0NW
Tel: 017684 82394 Fax: 017684 82034

Accommodation details:

Conveniently situated for Ullswater. There are large grounds and river frontage to the Goldrill Beck. Opens mid-February (but closed Wednesday and Thursday until Easter). Open daily thereafter until December, but closed Thursday during September and October and also Wednesday after October. Hostel open all day. Dinner served at 19.00.

Getting there:

Situated just south of Patterdale village, off the A592, leading to the Kirkstone Pass. By bus: take the 108 (from Penrith bus or train station), except Sundays.

Description:

Built in the style of a Scandinavian chalet in 1970. A very popular youth hostel offering a high level of comfort. Much of the roof is flat and covered with grass to blend the building into the scenery when viewed from above! The interior consists of pine woodwork giving a unique atmosphere. Mostly eight-bedded rooms, but there are also some two bedded. Very good drying room plus washing and drying machines for clothes. The big peaks such as Helvellyn, Fairfield and High Street are all accessible from here as well as many low level walks and the lake.

Skiddaw House YH

Bassenthwaite, Keswick, Cumbria CA12 4QX
Tel: Contact Carrock Fell YH 016974 78325

Accommodation details:

Situated at 1,550ft above sea level on the side of Skiddaw. One of the most isolated houses in England. Open between Easter and the end of October. Opens at 17.00 with a wet-weather shelter prior to this. This is the highest youth hostel in the UK.

Getting there:

On foot only!
By bus: Stagecoach Cumberland X5; Wright 888 from Penrith. Alight at Thelkeld. The hostel is 4.5 miles (7.2km) away. Cars may be parked at Fell carpark, Blease Road near Thelkeld or at Lattrigg near Keswick.

Description:

A former shooting lodge and once a pair of shepherd's cottages, with only limited facilities. No showers, very basic foodstore (self-catering only); no heating in dormitories, 24 volt lighting only, credit cards not accepted. Postal service is poor, so book well ahead or telephone Carrock Fell YH which has a CB link with Skiddaw House. There is room for 15 people in three rooms, but in this remote location, no one is turned away!
Although isolated, the hostel is comfortable with hot and cold running water, flush toilets, an effective drying room and a self-catering kitchen described as "rustic but well-equipped and spacious".

Thirlmere YH

The Old School, Stanah Cross, Keswick, Cumbria CA12 4TQ
Tel: 017687 73224

Accommodation details:

Formerly the village school for Legburthwaite. This is a small youth hostel offering limited facilities and accommodation in three dormitories. Open from Easter to early November but closed Mondays (and Tuesdays out of the main season). Opens at 17.00 with dinner served at 18.00 (please book meals in advance).

Getting there:

By bus: Stagecoach No 555 from Keswick or Windermere. Situated close to the junction of the B5322 and the A591 near the northern end of Thirlmere.

Description:

A single storey wooden building with few modern facilities such as carpets or TV! The dormitories can be a little chilly out of the main season. Situated at the side of the B5322. Off road carparking is limited to only a few vehicles.

Wast Water YH

Wasdale Hall, Wasdale, Seascale, Cumbria CA20 1ET
Tel: 09467 26222

Accommodation details:

This lovely half-timbered house (Wasdale Hall) dates from 1829. It is furnished in period style with many original features. Open for most of year, but closes Tuesday and Wednesday when open in the off-season. Open 17.00 but customer's kitchen/dining room open all day. Dinner served 19.00.

Getting there:

From the south: leave the M6 at Junction 36 and take the A590 to Greenodd; turn right onto the A595 to just past Broughton-in-Furness where you can take the fell road at Duddon Bridge to Eskdale. Follow the signs to Santon Bridge where you turn right for Wasdale. The hostel is 1 mile past Nether Wasdale down a track on the right.
From the north: leave the M6 at Junction 40, take the A66 to bypass Cockermouth, turn right onto the A5086 to Egremont and then onto the A595 to Gosforth. Turn left and follow the signs to Wasdale. The hostel is 1 mile past Nether Wasdale down a track on the right.
From the Central Lakes: if coming over Wrynose and Hardknott passes from Ambleside, please allow plenty of time as the road is often impassable in winter due to ice and slow going in summer due to the very heavy levels of traffic on what is only a single track road. By bus: Stagecoach Cumberland 12, Whitehaven-Seascale (passes close to Seascale Railway Station). Alight at Gosforth (5 miles, 8km away).

Description:

This is a lovely hostel built in pink granite with grounds extending down to the lake shore. The lounge has a magnificent carved open fireplace with a library of over 3,000 books. There are a few family-sized rooms, and cots and high chairs are available (if booked in advance). The building was refurbished a few years ago.

Windermere YH

High Cross, Bridge Lane, Troutbeck, Windermere, Cumbria LA23 1LA
Tel: 015394 43543 Fax: 015394 47165

Accommodation details:

This large house stands in an elevated position near Troutbeck village, 2 miles (3.2km) from Windermere. It is open for most of the year, closing for a few weeks at the end of the year. It opens at 13.00 and dinner is served at 19.00.

Getting there:

From Windermere follow the A591 north for one mile to Troutbeck Bridge. Take the first right turn beyond the filling station. The hostel is almost a mile up the lane on the left. By bus: There are frequent services to Ambleside. Alight at Troutbeck Bridge. The YHA bus may also be taken to this point from Windermere Railway Station. By rail: Windermere Station 2 miles (3.2km) away.

Description:

A large house in extensive grounds with spectacular views of Lake Windermere and the mountains beyond. The hostel is comfortably furnished and has many small rooms ideal for families. Troutbeck itself is one of the most attractive villages in Lakeland, famous for its beautiful seventeenth century farmhouses and many lovely walks.

HOSTELLING
INTERNATIONAL

Let us take the hassle out of planning your visit to the Lake District with the Lake District Reservations Service and YHA Shuttlebus Service

Use the Lake District Reservations Service to book your stay at any Youth Hostel in the Lake District up to seven days in advance. When you arrive the YHA Shuttlebus offers:

- *Free* transfer from Windermere railway station and National Express bus stop to Windermere and Ambleside Youth Hostels

- *Daily** door-to-door service to Youth Hostels in some of the best parts of Lakeland

- Rucksack transfer service — so you can really enjoy your walk

The only thing we can't organise is the weather !

*The YHA Shuttlebus currently operates from March-October

For more information on these and other YHA services in the Lake District
Tel: 015394 32304 (YHA Ambleside)
For Lake District Reservations Tel: 015394 31117

Notes

Notes

Free YHA Membership!

On production of the voucher (at the foot of this page) the owner of this book is entitled to free adult membership of the YHA for one year. Membership of the YHA enables you to hostel at any of the 240 Youth Hostels in England & Wales or any of the 5,000 in over 60 countries around the world. There are also many associated membership benefits including a valuable discount booklet, an annual guide to the hostels and a regular members magazine with news and articles. Remember that the YHA is a democratic organisation and membership also entitles you to take part in the way the Association is run. Membership can be obtained at the hostel you first stay at, through our National Office at St Stephen's Hill, St Albans, Herts, AL1 2DY (01727 855215)

Voucher: YHA - Free Membership Offer

Please complete in block capitals

Title (Mr/Mrs/Ms/Miss)   ....

First Names   ....

Surname   ....

Address   ....

....

Postcode   ....   Telephone No   ....

Date of Birth   ....

Signed ....
